Perspectives on Worship
52 stories, thoughts & insights
volume 1

Danielle,

Blessings on your own

Blessings on your own

soon Follow His will.

Zeph
3:17

Perspectives on Worship
52 stories, thoughts & insights
volume 1

Ken Abraham, Mike Atkins, Drew Cline, Lea Collins,
Dr. David C. Cooper, David M. Edwards, Jeff Ferguson,
Audra Almond-Harvey, Mark Hodge, Dallas Holm,
Lawrence Kimbrough, Laurie Klein, Greg Long, Babbie Mason,
Reba Rambo-McGuire, Gordon Mularski, Caleb Quaye, Harlan Rogers,
Dan Scott, Kathy Shooster, J. Daniel Smith, Sue Smith, Angel Smythe,
Kimberlee Stone, Regi Stone, and Patrick Tharp.
Edited by Lea Collins

EXPERIENCE WORSHIP

Thanks to each contributing author for sharing the perspectives that created this book: Ken Abraham, Mike Atkins, Drew Cline, Lea Collins, Dr. David C. Cooper, David M. Edwards, Jeff Ferguson, Audra Almond-Harvey, Mark Hodge, Dallas Holm, Lawrence Kimbrough, Laurie Klein, Greg Long, Babbie Mason, Reba Rambo-McGuire, Gordon Mularski, Caleb Quaye, Harlan Rogers, Dan Scott, Kathy Shooster, J. Daniel Smith, Sue Smith, Angel Smythe, Kimberlee Stone, Regi Stone, and Patrick Tharp.

Special thanks to David M. Edwards for his assistance with the compilation, to Lawrence Kimbrough for the wealth of character sketches, and to Janice Pike & Kimberlee Stone for their masterful proof reading.

2814 Azalea Place   Nashville, TN 37204
866-859-7622   info@experienceworship.com
www.experienceworship.com

EXPERIENCE WORSHIP

Contents

Introduction

This book doesn't come with a 12 Easy Step Guarantee, or tell you 30 things to do for 30 days that result in you being 30% more successful at Christian worship.

Good things definitely come from plans and programs that are designed to produce specific results in fixed amounts of time – as long as those methods are used to create new, healthy habits and jumpstart active, permanent life changes. We aren't saying that those methods have no place. We're just letting you know that this book doesn't work that way.

This won't be news to anyone, but people don't naturally work according to formulas and prescribed methods. Who has ever fallen madly in love by following a manual for discovering the perfect mate? Who has ever become passionately consumed with a world changing idea by working through a "14 Steps to Changing the World" program? It sounds crazy in those contexts. Obviously the things closest to our hearts – our dreams, our aspirations, our relationships – don't work like efficiency models or strategic plans. That's just not how we're made.

We can learn to utilize higher efficiency plans to help us improve our time management skills, or implement parenting models to help us intentionally train our children in the way they should go, or use discipleship programs to help ensure that we don't develop malnourished new believers with severely imbalanced character. But those things only *help* us do what has to be done. They don't do anything for us; they aren't magic spells that work simply by pronouncing the words correctly.

Worship, *real worship*, doesn't work that way, either. There is no one-size-fits-all plan for accomplishing a successful, worshipful life. You can't master the secrets of worship from a training module or absorb them in a weekend course. Becoming a worshiper won't work like implementing a business model.

Very simply and basely put, worship is the experience of us relating (rightly) with God. Worship isn't just songs or the musical portion of a church service; it isn't just artistic expression or taking care of the poor; it isn't even just obedience or sacrifice. All of those things are part of it, but they aren't *it*.

Real worship is about LIFE, lived fully in the awareness of God – lived *with* God as much as for Him. It doesn't only involve happy emotions; it should happen right in the middle of being terrified, angry, and depressed. Real worship encompasses every aspect of how we live with other people and what we do with what we have. You can't accomplish it. You can't master it. You can't absorb it. You can't implement it. You have to live it. You have to *experience* it.

Experience happens on your first day of school when you walk up to a small stranger and introduce yourself to the new person you desperately want to be your friend.

Experience happens when you sit down in the driver's seat, put on just the right music, and pull out of the driveway by yourself for the first time.

Experience happens as you slurp back your first oyster and feel it jiggle down your throat; it happens as you're gulping all the water at your table with blurry eyes and a throbbing, burning mouth because you accidentally met wasabi.

Experience happens the first time you move away from home, the first time you leave your country, the first time you hold the tiny person you *made*.

Experience happens the first time someone rejects you, the first time your heart is broken, the first time someone close to you dies.

In the approachable wisdom of Mark Twain, "A man who carries a cat by the tail learns something he can learn in no other way."

As so many people have said, there truly is no substitute for experience. It's not just how we learn, or the result of big things that occur in our lives. It's what life *is*. That's how God made it. And it's how God made us.

Worship has so many facets, so many definitions, so many expressions and faces and forms. But ultimately, whatever else it is or isn't, it is meant to be an experience that's as real and potent and tangible as everything else in our lives.

The statement that "we were made for worship" probably isn't a new thought for anyone who picks up this book. But what does that really, truly mean?[1] How does that understanding shape our lives and form our identities? What does it look like first thing in the morning when we wake up; at our first break in the workday; during the last waking hours of the night; as we brush our teeth to go to bed? What does it mean in our decision making? What does it mean in our relationships? *How* do we experience worship?

This book is about *that*. It probably doesn't have all the answers to all of your questions but it does have exactly what the title promises: perspectives on worship in the form of stories, thoughts, and insights in 52 article-style readings. It's written by 26 (mostly) normal people who are learning to live their lives as worship and are working out exactly what that means in their very different stations in life.

This book isn't revolutionary; it doesn't contain any new or secret knowledge. It's not the next best thing since sliced bread or washing machines. It probably won't singlehandedly change your life.

But...

if you truly desire worship to be your lifestyle, not just part of your church service;

if you want worship to be a practical, attainable, not-just-musical experience that's part of your everyday life in your everyday world;

if you are committed to finding practical ways to free worship from an exclusively musical context, to doing more than singing about how worship is more than a song;

if you are the sort of person who takes responsibility for actively making the changes in your life that God asks you to make, rather than expecting things to just happen to you or be handed to you pre-processed and easy to swallow;

if any of those sound familiar, then this book was made for you.

---

1 When we say that "we were made for worship," we very literally mean that the experience of worship is what we were made for; it's our purpose; it's built into the identity of humanity. We were created from the breath of God and the dust of earth, branded with the image and likeness of God Himself, and given the ability to live in relationship with Him – as real and tangible a relationship as that of the first husband and wife. From the very beginning God walked with them, talked with them, interacted with them in their everyday space in the most natural way possible. The story gets a little sour but never completely goes bad: God never abandoned us or changed His purpose for us. The entire Old Testament is a story of God's relentless pursuit to restore that relationship – God even made the first sacrifice to cover human sin and shame. Our restoration was completed with Jesus, which means that there is NOTHING Adam and Eve had access to that we're missing. There is nothing keeping us from that closeness, that relationship which takes place in our everyday space. That's where God has always wanted to be: right in the middle of every aspect of our lives. That, in a nutshell, is what we mean when we say "we were made for worship."

Using This Book

If you picked up this book to read through on your own, you might want to skip this section and carry on.

If you plan to use this as a resource in a small group setting and want some ideas on how to utilize it, this might be helpful for you.

This book contains 52 readings, but that number in the title isn't meant to be binding or restrict you in any way. There's nothing magical that happens when it's read once a week. It's structured with 52 readings for ease of use in a group setting because many groups get together once a week. But it can just as easily be read straight through or a few entries at a time. You can skip some or choose your favorites to make this a shorter study. Feel free to be creative in your usage.

This book was designed to be worked through in community. You can certainly read it any way you wish, but the intent is to give small groups of people – worship teams, Bible studies, Sunday school classes, home groups, families – a resource for exploring worship together. We have discovered that while most people agree that worship is "more than a song," it is very difficult to find people who talk about worship non-musically, let alone places where nonmusical elements are recognized as genuine expressions of worship (except, perhaps, for tithe and offering time). The goal with this book is to get you talking about not-*just*-musical worship and to provide some simple but slightly out of the ordinary ideas to put it into action.

These articles are meant to be accessible, touchable. They try to only use words that are easy to wrap your head around, words that aren't overly "Christian" sounding. They're words that make sense in the middle of everyday life, words you would use while washing dishes or playing with your children or spending your lunch break with a friend.

There are 26 different authors of the articles in this book. Each one sounds a little different. Some are experienced writers; some are used to public speaking or performing and are writing for the first time. Some cite The Message, some prefer the King James. Some tell stories, some offer short teaching snapshots, and some of them just sort of talk on paper. Some of them you'll recognize; many of them you won't. All of them offer perspectives from real people learning to live their lives as worship. Some of them probably wouldn't agree on fine theological points if they were to spend enough time together. But those things are all natural – and healthy – reflections of the real-life Body of Christ.

You won't find specific words to pray at the end of an article, or a bulleted list of "take away" thoughts. In this respect, we've leaned on the tradition of devotional classics like Oswald Chambers' *My Utmost for His Highest* and C.H. Spurgeon's *Morning and Evening*. Those authors didn't point out the things their readers should take away – and neither does the Bible, for that matter. They required the reader to interact with what was written, to meditate on it, to personally engage with what was most poignant to them. If they were going to pull anything lasting from those devotional works (as millions have done for nearly a century), the reader bore the responsibility of processing it into a "digestible" form for themselves. The authors provided the food for the reader to use to nourish themselves; they didn't attempt to present it pre-chewed so their readers had only to swallow it. There isn't any lasting reward in that, not much chance for change or character growth. The point of devotional time is investing yourself, really thinking on it, and allowing you and God together a chance to work out what you need to take from it. We didn't want to abort the thought process that an article might have begun by abruptly turning you in a preset direction.

What we *have* done is provide a section at the back of the book with article-specific ideas for application (Appendix 1). Each of the ideas allow for a combination of reflection, discussion, and experience. Many of them are good for all ages and mixed age groups. All of them aim to be down-to-earth and tangible.

If you are the group facilitator, this will require a little more work than some resources you'll find. To get the most out of it and be sure that it works for your group, you'll want to read the article and work through the action points ahead of time to be sure you know how to present it or alter it in ways that work best for your specific group. Some of them are more involved than others in their execution and will require letting your group know about them ahead of time (you might want to work through the whole list yourself before beginning this study with your group). Keep in mind that these are just suggestions to get you started. They aren't formulas or exclusive ways to hammer home the truth. Each group will be as different as each person who is in it. We've left blank space under each of our suggestions for you to write in your own ideas and make notes of what you actually did – what did and didn't work.

The most important thing is to make it real and participatory; to get people talking and thinking in honest, down-to-earth language; to break through the church versus real life barriers and allow worship to have its place right in the "normal" areas of our lives. God made us for life, not just church attendance, and He desires to share in every aspect of that life with us – not just the holy or sacred parts but *all* of it. When we learn to live our everyday experiences as worship – well, then we're *really* getting somewhere.

Welcome to the process.

Experiencing Worship
Lea Collins

That's the kind of people the Father is out looking for: those who are simply and honestly themselves before him in their worship.

~ Jesus

The setting is a rich pastureland of slightly rolling hills; a few trees dot the landscape. Grazing sheep are contentedly sprawled out a mile or so in every direction, filling the vale with the constant dull hum of their bleating. The air smells fresh, clean. A young teenage boy sits at the top of a small hill, almost lost among the sheep. He looks like my imaginary picture of Tom Sawyer or Huck Finn, eyes filled with big dreams and a mischievous craving for adventure. While the sheep are his responsibility and he cares for them well, he's usually lost in imagination.

When he isn't playing with the sheep or running around the fields, he's sitting under his tree, dreaming the adventures he'll have somewhere, sometime. Music and poetry are the language of this boy's soul, thus his dreams often become songs. There aren't always words. Sometimes he plays the song of the sheep, or the song of the creek, or the story of the bear attack he fended off. He doesn't play because he was told to – most of the time no one else is even around. He plays because there is music in him, because it *is* him.

As you've probably guessed, the boy is David, a personal hero for many of us. David became a very powerful and important man but he never lost what he learned as a teenager out with his sheep. Somehow, between the days outside alone and his unhindered hours of musical revelry, young David met God. He didn't only know about Him but he knew *HIM*, as few people have since. Understanding the character of God and what brings Him pleasure the way David did gave him tremendous insight into worship, insight that has set the tone for worship in Jewish and Christian communities ever since.

What really strikes me is the naturalness of it. That boy in the hills with his homemade instruments didn't play because it was required, or because that's what people did, or because he couldn't think of anything else to do. He did it because it was natural for him, because it was in his heart, because it was who he was. What came out was always completely honest – nothing feigned, nothing forced. Sometimes it was reflective. Sometimes it was exultant. Sometimes it was ugly, angry, and depressing. It all came out in his worship, which we have record of in the Psalms. Wherever he was, whatever he had, he brought it to God in music, the expression that was most natural to him.

There's a key in that for us. We spend so much time trying to discern what new and difficult thing we can do for God, what tough choice and painful sacrifice might bring Him the greatest glory and do the most to advance the Kingdom. Yet so often God is waiting and longing for us to do the easiest, most natural things we can do. We know that obedience is better than sacrifice but we often expect obedience to be as painful and hard and unnatural as the sacrifices.

One of my favorite quotes is from Eric Liddel, the Olympic gold medalist on whom the movie *Chariots of Fire* is based. In a newspaper interview, he said "God made me fast, and when I run I feel His pleasure." I love that because it makes worship seem so simple, so practical, so attainable. The deep, secret truth is that it really is.

This is worship: to do what we were created for, to be who we really are and share that experience with God. Living lifestyles of worship involves not only learning who God is and what makes Him happy but also learning who God has made us to be and being *that*, as strongly and fully as we can. Sometimes it leads us to hard places where every ounce of our character is tested and strained to its max. Sometimes it brings us to fiery places where we are completely turned inside out and disoriented with no idea who we are anymore. But sometimes it isn't hard or painful. Sometimes it's as simple as sitting on a hill making up songs when nobody is listening, just because there's music in our hearts.

What is the song in your soul? What makes you radiate with life? God put that in you and He desperately wants you to turn that back out as worship.

Play your music. Write your songs. Run as fast as you can. When you do, you'll feel His pleasure. And *that* is an experience of worship.

Why Do We Worship?

Dan Scott

The full union, of course,
is coming.
We rehearse for the wedding
now through worship.

~ John Eldredge

A few years ago, I heard a guy on the radio mock the notion of worship. He said that if we are to believe what the Bible says about God, we must necessarily come to the conclusion that God has a pathological need for compliments. In other words, God must delight in hearing us say, "Nice world you made, God" or "How swell of you to make the beaches over in Hawaii." God must also be incredibly worried about his rival to get so overjoyed hearing us describe what a jerk the Devil is. In this view, worship is a great pep rally – "Yea God! Go, go, go!" and "Down with the Devil! Booooo!"

The guy's comments stayed with me for a long time and bothered me. I mean, why *does* God need our worship? What could worship from the likes of us possibly do for the Creator of the universe? We live for seventy years on the average. We have enough brain capacity to eke out an existence, even to invent a few things before death comes and turns our lights out. Most of us will quit learning anything significant by the time we are twenty-five. Most of us will rarely contemplate much on the meaning of life or even our hope for eternal existence. We will work, sleep, mate, eat, get old, and die.

God, on the other hand, has such infinite intelligence that He knows *everything* – everything that has been, everything that will be, everything that is, and even everything that could be but is not. What joy could a God like that possibly get from hearing us gather once a week and sing or say something to the effect of "For He's a jolly good fellow, which nobody can deny?"

No, if we look at worship as something that God needs, then we must seriously consider that the impious remarks the guy made on the radio make a lot of sense. Obviously, God does not call us to worship because He needs our adoration. He calls us to worship because we need to adore Him. Worshiping is not something God needs, it is something *we* need.

We Christians believe that we have been caught up into the love of God. Now we don't know *why* He loves us but we believe that He *does*. Because He does, He has chosen to transform us into a new kind of creature, much like the old story of Geppetto and Pinocchio.

- Why Do We Worship? -
Dan Scott

8

Pinocchio, you remember, was a wooden puppet who wanted to be a real boy. Like him, we want to be changed. We are presently temporal and limited beings but we long to be eternal, to "put on divine nature," as St. Peter puts it in his little epistle. Not only do we want that but, evidently, God wants it, too, and worship is the process by which it happens. As we worship, we begin to become like Him, to put on His divine nature.

Worship has three main ingredients that call us to a higher order of being: transcendence, community, and transformation.

Transcendence is the quality of worship that alerts our spirit that we are in a different environment than the bank or Wal-Mart. It is what we call "awe," that sometimes scary part of worship that can make our hair stand up on end and remind us that we are creatures of eternity. When worship is transcendent, we recall that *"this world is passing away and all it contains but he who does the will of God lives forever."* (1 Jn 2:17, NIV)

Community is the part of worship that we acknowledge with the first word of the Lord's Prayer – "Our." By saying Our Father, we are recognizing the fact that we have spiritual siblings. So we pass the peace, or give a hearty handshake, or hug someone's neck. Worship is not only about God. It is also about recognizing our neighbor.

Transformation is about deep, radical change. It is about seeking to leave behind the pettiness and sinfulness of life and choosing to walk in the ways of God.

In worship, we hear the scripture read and preached, we enter the presence of God, and we pray for transformation. That's why we worship: to become like the Lord. That's why He invites us to worship: not because He needs it, but because we do.

Lift Your Eyes

Drew Cline

Worship is a way of seeing the world in the light of God.

~ Abraham Joshua Heschel

The human heart is a funny thing. Mine seems to be on some sort of rollercoaster most days, from the exhilarating heights of adventure and dreams made reality all the way to the valleys of despair and self-doubt. My emotions can run the gamut from thankfulness to selfishness within a beat of my heart.

Sometimes I think it's because I'm an artist. We're supposed to be melancholy and moody, in touch with our feelings yet possessing the clarity to write about them or make that feeling translate somehow through a piece of music. History tells us that musicians used to be considered crazy and were often put in mental institutions. That seems a little harsh, but then again, I've met some pretty wacky musicians...

I'm not bi-polar; I'm *human*. We all face struggles and joys that cause our hearts to feel up and down, happy and sad, or plain worn out. But those of us who follow Jesus don't have to just try and hang on for the ride. Instead, we trust that there's a hand hanging on to us.

I remember riding with a friend through some winding roads one time when I began to feel sick. My head was spinning and my stomach was following suit. My friend said, "Look out the front window and find something to look at, something a long ways away, and focus on it." He said, "If you stay focused on it, it will calm your mind and stomach and you won't be focused on the rough terrain." I tried it, and to my amazement it worked!

I've now found myself giving that advice to people when I'm driving them around. Somehow focusing on that one steady object can help you feel better. I'm reminded of Peter who enthusiastically called out to Jesus, "If it's You, allow me to come to You on the water." Jesus agrees and Peter hops out of an already rocky boat onto a turbulent sea. He starts walking but that old 'rough terrain' starts to get to him. He looks up and calls to Jesus, "Save me!" Jesus reaches out and asks, "Why did you take your eyes off of Me?"

There's no doubt in my mind that you, like me and every other person on the planet, can get down, feel depressed, hopeless, alone, lost, and confused (you can add your own list of struggles and miseries here). There will be days when we feel our spirits beginning to crash and burn, days when our unrealized dreams throw us into a tail spin. Remember the encouraging words from Psalm 121 to "lift your eyes." Don't let the stuff of this world cause your heart's focus to blur and your spirit to be crushed. Instead, raise your head, lift your eyes (physically and spiritually), pull your focus off yourself, change your countenance, take a deep breath in God's grace, and, like Peter, call out. Jesus will hear you, He will come to you, and He will be the calm in your storm.

Sometimes it takes a while for us to focus, but once you've found that place of peace and strength in Jesus, stay there. Don't rush that moment. Trust that He will be all you need for whatever struggle you face. Allow Him to settle your spirit and give you strength. He promised He would do it.

Do you need to stop for a while to focus on Him, on His plan for your life, on His goodness? Don't let your busy day keep you from His peace.

Abraham

Lawrence Kimbrough

Worship was nothing new to Abraham. In his ancient Mesopotamian homeland, worship was everywhere. Worship of the sun, the moon, the stars, of any force in nature that escaped the harness of human control.

Abraham knew how to worship. He'd just never had a god start the conversation before.

But this one talked. And gave directions. *"Go out from your land, your relatives, and your father's house, to the land that I will show you. I will make you into a great nation, I will bless you, I will make your name great, and you will be a blessing." (Gen 12:1-2, HCSB)*

Unheard of.

So who knows what drove Abraham to obey such an irrational request. He'd already lugged his family and possessions nearly 800 miles from home, moving with his daddy's people from Ur to Haran. Surely, he thought, his traveling days were over.

But maybe at 75 he had been starting to think deeper thoughts than usual, wondering what life was all about, seeing through the silly, superstitious charades of his own pagan worship. Perhaps he was longing to latch onto something real. A god who was bigger than the fickle ones he knew. A god like this invisible one.

So he did it. He pulled up stakes and headed south into the giant-infested countryside of Canaan. There he built an altar "and called on the name of the LORD." That was the way you did it, see? That was the way you worshiped. Only this time, it felt different inside. Genuine. This god, this capital-G god, was taking an interest in him. Unlike the silent, stoic gods of moon and sky, this God seemed to love him, to enjoy his company, to appreciate his worship. So as God continued to speak, Abraham continued building altars and offering worship.

Until one day when his worship went beyond curiosity…and became belief.

Abraham had been trying hard to believe God's promises of nations and power, of descendants as numerous as the dust on the ground. But there was this one little problem. How hard can it be to count to zero? As in zero children? No son. No heir. No way for the promise to come true.

So Abraham decided to approach God in a way he'd never done before – in a way no other god reportedly allowed. He approached Him like a friend, like someone who didn't mind being bothered by honest questions. *"LORD God, what will you give me, seeing I go childless?" (Gen 15:2, NKJV)*

Like a naughty dog bracing for the pop of a rolled-up newspaper, perhaps Abraham squinted through shaking fingers into the silent darkness of his tent, thinking himself the foolish culprit of an unforgivable affront.

But the answer returned. Not angrily, not with fire, yet with the firm resolve of a God who was really in charge: *"One who will come from your own body shall be your heir." (Gen 15:4, NKJV)*

Then, as if laying a fatherly arm across Abraham's shoulder, pushing back the tent flap with the other, and pointing with an outstretched hand into the heavens, God said, *"Count the stars if you are able to number them...so shall your descendants be." (Gen 15:5, NKJV)*

And something clicked in Abraham that night. As the writer of Genesis put it, *"He believed in the LORD, and [God] accounted it to him for righteousness." (Gen 15:6, NKJV)*

The apostle Paul would later turn that one verse into his strongest argument for the triumph of grace over law. Abraham believed. He didn't run twenty-five laps around the altar, didn't dust his head in ashes, didn't sell all he had and give it to the poor.

He just believed.

Believed enough to endure the twenty-five year gap between a laughable promise and its improbable fulfillment. Believed enough to endure the pain of circumcision at 99 years of age. Believed enough to gather wood and fire and climb numbly with Isaac to the top of Mount Moriah, not knowing that God was leading a ram step for step up the other side.

An eternal covenant had been born through belief. And belief had been born in worship.

The Heart of Worship
Mike Atkins

In the Old Testament, God took pleasure in the many sacrifices of worship because they foretold of Jesus' sacrifice for us on the cross. Now God is pleased with different sacrifices of worship: thanksgiving, praise, humility, repentance, offerings of money, prayer, serving others, and sharing with those in need.
Real worship costs.

~ Rick Warren

Worship is such a hot topic today.

We talk about styles of worship. We talk about methods of worship. We talk about ancient/modern worship. We talk about contemporary versus traditional worship. There is the hymn crowd and the alternative crowd, emerging worship and sacramental worship.

We gear services towards worship styles in order to tailor worship to the needs of the congregation. Worship music comes in all flavors. The volume of worship music being produced annually allows for a treasure trove of options for the modern worshiper.

But in all of the debate, discussion, and experimentation, I wonder if perhaps we have forgotten what the heart of worship was really meant to be. The heart of worship is not found in styles, rhythms, or cadence. Nor is it found in lyrics, orchestrations, or multi-media presentations. The heart of worship from Genesis to Revelation has always been summed up in one word: *SACRIFICE*.

In the Old Testament, sacrifice and worship were inseparable terms. Worship *was* sacrifice. Worship involved the stoking of fires and the shedding of blood as much as the sound of trumpets and the singing of songs. The worshipers of the Old Testament came to honor God, to be cleansed of their sin by blood and to offer sacrifices to a holy God. Their worship was prescribed, not by their personal taste or style of interest, but by the needs of their spiritual condition and by the righteous requirements of God's character. Worship was a sacrifice. It wasn't for the worshiper. It was for God.

It was a sacrifice to bring a lamb to the altar. It was a sacrifice to confess sin. It was a sacrifice to lay hands on the head of the lamb and transfer guilt. It was a sacrifice to keep the fire burning on the altar. Worship was not play. It was work. It was the work of righteousness, of maintaining a right relationship with God.

Is it possible that we focus too often on the musicality of worship and forget that in scripture the songs of worship were the by-product of a heart that had worshiped God aright: through offering the sacrifices that worship required?

- The Heart of Worship -
Mike Atkins

20

Praise comes naturally out of a heart that has been forgiven. Lament flows naturally out of a heart that has been convicted. Songs of love flow naturally out of a heart that has been accepted, after confession and prayer, into the Father's grace-filled arms. Where sacrifice has occurred, worship follows. Style matters little then. It is the condition of the heart that makes the difference. Conversely, the most fitting style and expert musical expression cannot move a heart that has not experienced sacrifice.

It could be argued that sacrifice is no longer a relevant term for the New Testament worshiper. Some might suggest that Christ's sacrifice was the end of sacrifice and therefore ends also the role of sacrifice in worship. Those who argue such should not forget that the New Testament calls upon believers to offer the sacrifice of praise as well as ourselves as living sacrifices.

What, then, is sacrifice in the New Testament sense? King David once remarked to someone who offered him a "free" sacrifice; *"I will not sacrifice to the LORD my God burnt offerings that cost me nothing." (2 Sam 24:24, NIV)* David understood that at the heart of any true act of worship there is a cost, a sacrifice.

In the New Testament the cost is more subtle than that of bulls and goats, of shekels, wine and grain. The sacrifices required are a contrite heart and a broken spirit as David declared, but there is also the sacrifice of enduring an imperfect style in church and yet finding God in the imperfections of man. There is the sacrifice of worshiping next to those who have disappointed you or wounded you and finding the grace of God to forgive them and hold their hand in heartfelt thanks. There is the sacrifice, dare I say it, of singing a song with a style that does not "move" you but with a message that is consistent with the common faith of all who call upon God's mercy and grace because of Jesus.

Perhaps in essence the sacrifice of praise means an attitude that does not demand that all worship conform to a musical signature that fits the worshiper, but rather that calls the worshiper to the uncomfortable act of self-denial, that evokes a price of honest exposure and forgiveness of sin, resulting in a sacrifice of personal preference on the altar of personal change.

With all the buzz about worship styles, perhaps we should revisit the real point of worship. Worship happens wherever man meets God, a sacrifice is offered up (whether ours in humility and self-denial, or Christ's in celebration and appreciation) and a life is changed.

Less than that is just singing songs.

Diving In
Audra Almond-Harvey

Wonder is the basis of worship.

~ Thomas Carlyle

God is big.

This concept is important to grasp – that no matter what understanding we have, God is bigger. No matter what suffering we endure or how unfair life is, God is bigger. No measurement exists to define Him, nothing can contain Him. He placed the heavens and the earth and has *"weighed each mountain and hill."* (Is 40:12, MSG) Who is His equal?

And yet, this same God sent His Son to us, that we might come to Him. Though *"all Lebanon's forests cannot supply sufficient fuel, nor all its wild beasts furnish victims enough to burn sacrifices worthy of the Lord"* (Is 40:16, AMP), He wants us to be close to Him. He loves us so much He gave His Son to die and live again that we might be able to come to Him.

So on the one hand, He is big. On the other hand, He desires intimacy with us. His majesty is overwhelming, and yet He wants us to come to Him like little children. How can this work?

A child approaches very big things quite differently than adults do, as my son reminded me when we went to the beach recently. We walked up to the shoreline, his eyes huge. It is a rare moment when he doesn't have something to say, but here, he was silent for several minutes. Then he looked up at me and said, "Mommy, that's *awesome*," dropped what he was carrying, took off his shoes, and ran into the water.

To children, nearly everything is bigger than they are. So the fact that the ocean is bigger than my son came as no surprise to him. He was in awe because the ocean was bigger than anything else he had seen. But he quickly discovered something just as cool as its size: you can splash in it. You can dig your feet into the sand, and find shells of animals that you never see on dry land. The waves go over your head. The seaweed tickles your toes. You can immerse yourself in it.

The next day, he didn't want to eat breakfast. He didn't want any of his toys, and he didn't even notice the television. He put on his swimsuit and his sandals and was waiting downstairs for me, having just dumped sunscreen all over himself as well as the floor. He could barely hold still.

- Diving In -
Audra Almond-Harvey

When we got to the beach, there was no waiting patiently at the shore. He had his shoes off and was in the water before I could even unload my arms. When it was time to go, he cried, and waved bye-bye sadly. That night he thanked God for making the ocean, and sand, and buckets to make sandcastles.

Once he had discovered how awesome the ocean was, he didn't care about doing anything else. He can't even wrap his head around how big the ocean really is, but he knows it's big and overwhelming; that it's beautiful, but sometimes scary. If we could remember how we saw the world when we were children, it would be much easier to understand how to come to the Father.

The disparity between God's hugeness and our comparative smallness is there only for adults. As adults, we think that since we have grown up we are no longer small. The world can be conquered. We admire God and His power. We desire His strength. We want to stand next to Him, to get all the benefits from faith in our lives. But this is the admiration of one who has forgotten you can never get big enough to be like God. We give Him His twenty minutes, or five, or the drive to church on Sunday with the kids screaming in the backseat, and we wonder why He seems so far away.

How many of our difficulties relating to God would remain if we still understood how to let experiences consume us? If we truly understood how big He is, we would have no problems making time to be with Him. Food wouldn't be nearly as important, and who cares about TV? The Creator of the universe is in the room, waiting to be with us! What else is essential?

He does not desire for us to simply stand there, and look at His hugeness, and keep ourselves dry on the shore. Experience isn't always clean or predictable. It can even be scary. But we are safe inside Him, even though we don't understand how.

So dive in!

Holy Rain
Regi Stone

At the end of the day, when I am lying in bed and I know the chances of any of our theology being exactly right are a million to one, I need to know that God has things figured out, that if my math is wrong we are still going to be okay.

Wonder is that feeling we get when we let go of our silly answers, our mapped out rules that we want God to follow.

I don't think there is any better worship than wonder.

~ Donald Miller

Growing up in the South, we always referred to a slow rain as a sprinkling. Others called it a mist or a drizzle. Whatever you call it, it gets everything wet. If you watch the grass or a bed of flowers during a sprinkling, it seems like the flowers take on a different personality. And the grass seems to spring to attention as if the rain has somehow caused it to realize its full potential.

I love the rain. I love to listen to the rain. When I was eight years old my grandparents lived in an old farm house surrounded by pecan trees and gnats. There were many afternoons when the sky produced clouds and an afternoon shower. After a shower the evening became muggy or cool, depending on the time of year. But one thing was certain at any time of year: the rain changed everything. There was nothing quite like sitting on my grandparents' front porch in their old gray wooden swing, listening as the rain poured onto the tin roof. Years later, I still enjoy a good rain. Not the kind that comes with harsh winds, thunder, and lightning, but the gentle kind: sprinklings, afternoon showers.

Sometimes I experience an altogether different kind of rain. I can't see it. I can't touch it. I can't smell it. But I can feel it. It permeates every nook and cranny of my being. I call it a holy rain. I don't know why, really. I guess because the same God who causes the rain outside to fall also has something to do with this rain as well, and it feels very similar.

Have you ever been in the middle of a bad or difficult situation where you didn't know what to do but then you felt calm around you? Have you ever experienced peace when your mind was in turmoil? I have, and it's really much like the rain in a way. If you imagine peace falling just like the rain, all around, soaking your entire being, bringing gentle comfort and unexplainable peace, that's the rain I'm talking about.

Growing up I used to hear people talk about God being right beside us. I wasn't really sure what that meant. Fortunately, my four-year-old son seems to grasp it better than I did. My wife recently told him that God is everywhere. The other night he had her look under the bed to see if God was there. He was so certain that God was there that he expected my wife to find Him under the bed or behind the door.

Many religious groups have their gods in clear sight so they can touch and see them. But we pray to and worship one who we can't see. We know, however, that when we pray or worship God, He smiles. There's also a little scripture well hidden in Zephaniah 3:17 that says God rejoices over us with singing. That's powerful. No other god makes that claim. The reality is He is always near us, longing for our conversation and worship. We need to have the ability, like my son, to feel certain at all times that God is right beside us.

When it rains these days I can't help thinking that God is blessing the earth so that it may flourish. That is exactly what He does in our lives. He rains down grace, mercy, faithfulness, healing, or whatever blessing He sees that we need. He is a gracious God who loves us more than we could ever imagine. Regardless of the circumstance, time of day or year, there is always something to give God thanks and praise for. And it's that belief, that awareness of His really being there, just as real as the rain, that allows His holy rain to soak our lives, helping us to reach our full potential.

Joseph

Lawrence Kimbrough

The Bible doesn't have a lot to say specifically about Joseph's experiences in worship. His is primarily a story of ironclad character, family loyalty, and revengeless restraint: heroic qualities that have secured him a noble name in religious history.

But in the final recorded test of his life, with his beloved father dead and his shell-shocked brothers still squirming to stay in his good graces, Joseph looked back over a confusing journey of abuse and injustice . . . and could see the hand of God. *"You meant evil against me,"* he said to his trembling brothers, *"but God meant it for good, in order to bring it about as it is this day, to save many people alive." (Gen 50:20, NKJV)*

So with his forgiving heart laid open – at a time when he had the cause, the license, and the means to unleash his justifiable wrath – he revealed something he never actually spoke, something another worshiper would later put in words for future generations: *"The LORD is my strength and my song, and He has become my salvation." (Psalm 118:14, NKJV)*

This was the kind of worship that defined Joseph, the kind of heart which held bitterness at bay. His tears surely fell in many places: the dusty bottom of a desert pit, the dank hollows of a prison cell, the lonely corners of a foreign land. But if he ever shook his fist into the Egyptian sky and cursed the God whose covenant required such pain and humiliation from him, you never hear of it.

Through it all, with no one around to encourage his system of belief, he worshiped deeply, though in silence. Unlike his legendary ancestors, he never admitted to having a face-to-face with the God of Abraham, Isaac, and Jacob. But the Bible says repeatedly, *"The LORD was with Joseph,"* showing him mercy, giving him favor, winning him success, sustaining his perspective through adversity and acclaim, revealing God's plan for moving His chosen people a generation closer to their destiny.

Where else could his great wisdom have come from, unless indeed *"the fear of the LORD is the beginning of wisdom" (Proverbs 9:10, NKJV)*, for Joseph had wisdom that other people could only dream about – even a pharaoh who pretended to be a god himself.

But worshiping the Lord had been Joseph's habit from childhood. Remember the first time you met Joseph? At a tender 17? The fair-haired favorite of his doting father, with a colorful imagination to match his colorful new coat? His timing was a little off, his discretion a little unseasoned, but his heart was exploding with revelations, of prophecies perhaps meant for his eyes only, but delivered overnight from a God wanting him to be accustomed to listening with his spirit.

And in learning how to listen to that voice, when every other voice inside him and around him was saying something different, he endured the whipping winds of change, maintained his integrity against the purring of Potiphar's wife, and deferred the glory to God even when taking credit for his own wisdom would have more predictably secured his prison release.

As evidenced by the naming of his children (Manasseh: For God has made me forget all my toil and all my father's house; Ephraim: For God has caused me to be fruitful in the land of my affliction), Joseph's worshipful spirit enabled him to lay the past in the grave of forgetfulness and be content with the fruit God had cultivated through his life, even if it had to be sown in affliction.

Worship had seen him through.

The Size of Our God &
The Size of Our Worship

Dallas Holm

The Church has surrendered
her once lofty concept of
God and has substituted
for it one so low, so ignoble,
as to be utterly unworthy of
thinking, worshipping men...

We have lost our spirit of
worship and our ability to
withdraw inwardly to meet
God in adoring silence.

~ A. W. Tozer

I am the Lord, and there is no other;
Besides Me there is no God...
The One forming light and creating darkness,
Causing well-being and creating calamity;
I am the Lord who does all these.

~ Isaiah 45:5,7 (NASB)

Our worship will only be as expansive as our concept of God. If God's all-encompassing greatness is diminished in any way in our minds, then so too will be our attempts to worship Him. If we think God is only involved in some areas, then we will only be involved in worship in some areas. There is always a direct correlation between the size of our God and the size of our worship. It is indeed significant that God, by His Holy Spirit, inspired Isaiah to write, *"The One forming light and creating darkness, causing well-being and creating calamity; I am the Lord who does all these." (Is 45:7, NASB)*

The first time God inspired a man to write down words on a manuscript He chose to give us the book of Job, scripture's oldest book. In the book of Job we immediately learn that both the treasures and the testing come from God. Job readily embraces this truth and proclaims, *"The Lord gave and the Lord has taken away. Blessed be the name of the Lord." (Job 1:21, NASB)*

I fear that much of our contemporary worship focuses only on certain aspects of God. We worship the parts of God we like; we sing and extol the virtues that bring us comfort and in the process we make God "smaller" and our worship is retarded. There is often a lightness, if not flippancy, evidenced in our forms of worship because we're only approaching the God of "light" and "well-being," not remembering the One who creates "darkness" and "calamity."

Jeremiah tells us that, *"When He utters His voice, there is a tumult of waters in the heavens, and He causes the clouds to ascend to the ends of the earth; He makes lightning...He brings out the wind from His storehouses." (Jer 10:13, NASB)* Nahum teaches us that, *"His way is in the whirlwind and the storm..." (Nah 1:3, NASB)* Our forms of worship often evidence the fact that we know little of this God of storms, lightning, darkness, and calamity, or if we do we're not too comfortable with Him. Remember His mercy is equal to His judgment, and His grace is equal to His wrath.

It is an elementary notion of this totally awesome God that can alone incite true worship. If "the fear of the Lord is the beginning of wisdom," then doesn't it follow that wise worship should include and involve a heavy dose of reverence for this awesome, sovereign God? So often our worship is self-centered more than God-centered. Next time you find yourself worshiping in song, count the "I's" and "me's" in much of our music and ask yourself, "Who am I really thinking about: Him or me?"

Paul gives us perhaps the clearest call to true worship in the book of Romans: *"Therefore, I urge you, brethren, by the mercies of God, to present your bodies a living and holy sacrifice, acceptable to God, which is your spiritual service of worship." (Rom 12:1, NASB)* More than forms, more than songs, more than time or finances but rather a literal giving of our very being to Him is what's required. A laying down of our bodies on the altar of sacrifice – "I must decrease, He must increase!"

The worship that will ascend to the heavens and be received as a sweet savor by a Holy God is less about the song and more about the singer. The sweetest note sounded in our Savior's ear will be the music of a life humbly and sacrificially lived for Him. With our best effort we could never pen nor sing so beautiful a note. It must be lived!

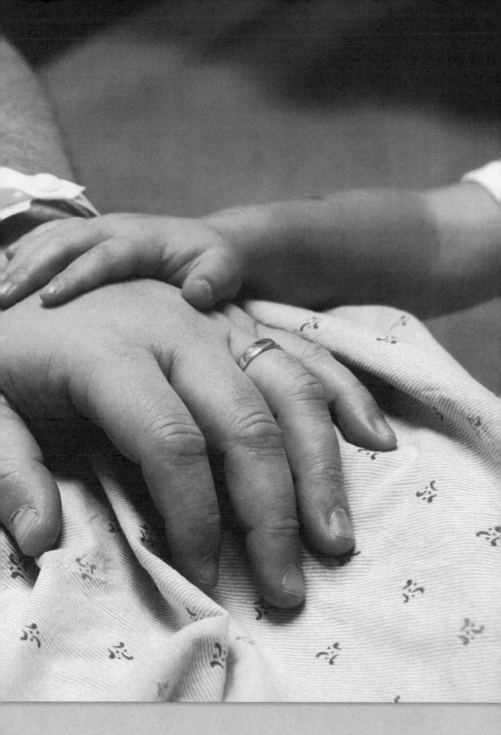

Circle of the Broken
Sue Smith

We're the walking wounded
No pretending we're all right
We meet to share the stories
Of our struggles in this life

And in the telling though there are tears
Something happens here

Words have offered comfort
Sometimes we've simply wept
And there is understanding
Though a lot is left unsaid

Cause in the silence love is the bond
We know we belong

In the circle of the broken
Where no one's heart is whole
In the middle of the hurting
We find hope
We fall upon God's mercy
We rest in grace
We're all sinners we're all saints
When the circle of the broken prays

Are you desperate, grieving
Filled with fear
You are welcome
You are needed here

~ Sue Smith & Kevin Stokes

I never thought I would be the kind of person who would be addicted to an online discussion board. Oh sure, I chat with friends on the Internet, and I even have an i-Sight camera that allows me to write with co-writers in other cities. But suggest I go into a chat room with people I don't know, and I just cringe.

But the truth is that for the past year, I've rarely let a day go by without checking the discussion board that is part of writeaboutjesus. com. On the board, people post lyrics and other people respond to them. We talk about silly things like reality TV and what our friends have posted in their blogs that day, and there are always posts about recording equipment and getting the most for your money in a home studio.

Then there are the prayer requests. There's a whole section of the board where people ask us to pray for their church, a friend who is ill, a sibling who is rebelling again the Lord – any number of things like that. Becky was one of the Write About Jesus people who always posted a response to every prayer request, promising to pray no matter what the request was.

I knew a little of Becky's story. She and her husband Steve had traveled and sung full-time with their son and daughter until about four years ago when their six-year-old, Sarah, was diagnosed with neuroblastoma, a deadly form of cancer that attacks young children. Sarah had gone through rounds of chemo and radiation and a bone marrow transplant, and as Becky posted on the board in her bio, they were rejoicing that Sarah had been in remission since last year.

One day during the summer, Becky asked us to pray for her daughter. Her teacher had noticed Sarah limping at school, and then she ran a high fever without any other symptoms of the flu or a cold. These were the very symptoms that preceded Sarah's original diagnosis. Dozens of people promised their prayer support, and we waited each day for Becky to post the latest on Sarah: her visit to the doctor, her tests at Duke University, waiting for the results of blood work and bone scans.

There was a very sad day when Becky let us know that the tests showed that Sarah had relapsed. Children who relapse with neuroblastoma, Becky said, are basically living on borrowed time. There is no cure. It is not a

- Circle of the Broken -

Sue Smith

42

question of whether they will die, but how quickly.

We continued to pray. If it is possible to cry with people over the Internet, that's what we did. I could actually feel the profound compassion people had for Sarah and her whole family. It was partly because Becky is a writer herself and would share with us in great detail what it was like to walk this road, armed only with an unwavering faith that God is good and that He is in control.

Throughout the summer we prayed. Of course, Sarah wasn't the only prayer request on our list. There was a family losing their business and faced with crushing financial problems. There was a church with a pastor who had left his family. There was someone's grandmother who had been abused in a nursing home and a friend whose children were having a rough time in school. We prayed for all of them.

Time after time I would see Becky's name on each discussion string. She wrote more than just "I'm praying for you." She wrote thoughtful, personal messages of love and encouragement, and I knew beyond any doubt that she was lifting up each name faithfully in her prayers.

I have to admit I wondered about that. If I had a child with cancer, would I spend any time praying for others, or would I spend every single second on my knees praying for her? Maybe that sounds selfish and even foolish, but I was constantly humbled and astonished by Becky's prayers for other people.

I looked up and down the list of those we were praying for... all of them praying right back for the others on the list. Not a single one of us had our act together. We were all just in need of God's help and of the prayers of the saints. A lyric began to be born in my heart and mind, a song about broken people praying each other through this life.

While a big part of our worship is praising God and telling Him how amazing He is, another part of it is simply saying, "I trust You, Lord. I believe You are who You claim to be. I believe You'll do what You say You'll do. I believe You are good. I believe You are loving. I believe You are in control."

This is worship: a circle of broken people, loving God, loving each other, lifting up each other's needs to the Father because we believe He can and will answer.

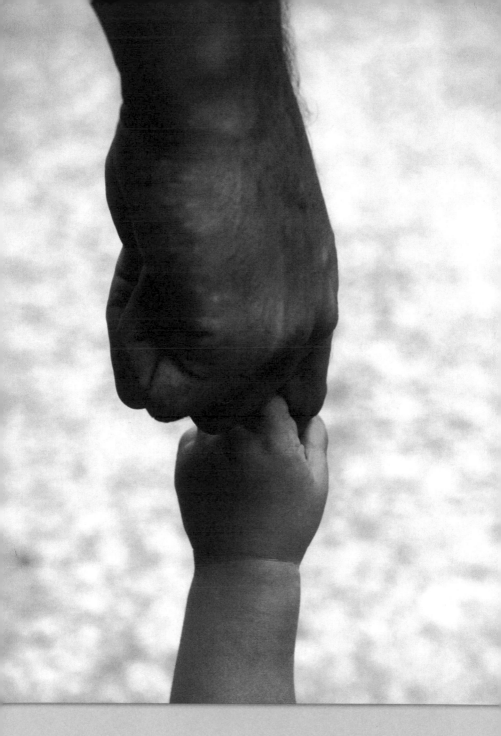

Friend of God

Kathy Shooster

Worship changes the worshiper
into the image
of the One worshiped.

~ Jack Hayford

"I am a friend of God," I sang in full voice, along with the thousands packed into the auditorium, hungry for the Lord's presence. As I meditated on this chorus written by songwriters/worship leaders Michael Gungor and Israel Houghton, I was challenged by what it means to be God's friend. The Holy One of Israel, our Creator and Redeemer, extends to us an awesome, indescribable invitation to be intimate with Him.

His knock at my heart's door created a deep spiritual hunger in me which provoked me to search for Him. Before I was a believer in Yeshua (Jesus), I was challenged by the Patriarchs' intimacy with God. Abraham was called God's friend and Moses spoke with God *"face to face, as a man speaks to his friend." (Ex 33:11, NKJV)* When Moses returned from spending forty days and nights with God upon Mt. Sinai, his face shone so much that the people of Israel couldn't look at him! Psalm 34:5 says, *"They looked to Him, and were radiant and their faces were not ashamed." (NKJV)* I longed to be so close to God that His presence would supernaturally change my countenance. How I yearned for that special bond with God!

The Lord's yearning for us cost Him everything. In order to bridge the gap between His holiness and our sinfulness, our heavenly Father gave His only Son, to sacrifice His life in order to atone for our iniquities.

"Greater love has no one than this, than to lay down one's life for his friends. You are my friends if you do whatever I command you. No longer do I call you servants, for a servant does not know what his master is doing; but I have called you friends, for all things that I heard from My Father I have made known to you." (Jn 15:13-15, NKJV)

For friends, there is no substitute for spending quality time together; it is mutual love that makes this a priority. Being together is paramount to everything else. In our fast-paced world we must make it a daily priority to steal away with the Lord. This may sound elementary; however, it is not enough to know about Him from what others say. We must know Him intimately and experience Him personally.

The Holy Spirit discloses a key to living by the Spirit of God in Amos 3:3: *"Can two walk together unless they are agreed?" (NKJV)* Friendship with God means our hearts are in agreement with His. As God's friends we are extended the opportunity to unite our hearts with the deepest desires of His heart.

King David said in Psalm 37:4: *"Delight yourself in the Lord, and He shall give you the desires of your heart." (NKJV)* There was a time in my walk with God when I understood this to mean that if I loved Him, He would give me the things I wanted. When this didn't happen I was confused and sorely disappointed. I asked God to show me what this verse really meant. How does one delight in the Lord? I discovered that as I took pleasure in Him by putting Him first, everything that I thought I wanted paled in comparison. His smile upon me became my greatest joy. His presence satisfied my deepest longing. His delight was the only thing that mattered to me.

Extraordinarily, He also transformed the desires of my heart. My self-centered desires no longer looked so attractive in the light of His glory and holiness. I discovered that He gave me new desires – designs for good, to give me a future and a hope (Jer 29:11).

As we draw closer to Him, He changes our hearts so that we are in harmony with Him. By God's grace we are His friends and family, accepted in the Beloved. The truth of who He is and what He has done for us delights and overwhelms us, igniting our worship. Our hearts cry out in adoration,

"Whom have I in heaven but You? And there is none upon earth that I desire besides You. My flesh and my heart fail; But God is the strength of my heart and my portion forever." (Ps 73:25-26, NKJV)

Moses

Lawrence Kimbrough

With the clear exception of Jesus Christ himself, no man ever enjoyed a more personal, intimate, worshiping relationship with God than Moses did.

"The LORD spoke to Moses face to face, as a man speaks to his friend" (Ex 33:11, NKJV), giving him exclusive access into the "consuming fire," the "thick darkness" of His glorious presence, not revealing His will through complex mysteries or shadowy visions, but by communicating with him "even plainly," eye to eye (Num 12:8, NKJV).

Yet if you'd told Moses a hundred years before that he would ever be on such intimate speaking terms with the one true God, he'd have said you were out of your mind.

You might have been able to convince him that he'd one day be a high-paid government official in Egypt. After all, as a young man he was enjoying a life of privilege and learning there, obtaining an insider's grasp of Egyptian beliefs and heritage. Had he known that not too far down the line he would discover the truth of his parentage, you might have even gotten him to concede he could wind up a fugitive, wasting away in poverty and anonymity on the backside of nowhere.

But never… *this.*

To imagine what he was to become, he would have had to see a bush burning in the distance among the shadows of Sinai, and hear a Voice calling to him from the middle of the flame. He would have had to feel the rush of dread that drove him to his knees but stirred a yearning desire for him to draw near to the God of his fathers. He would have had to sense the nervous strangeness of returning to his boyhood home in Egypt, stripped of the raw brashness he had known in his glory days decades before, yet watching raw power flow through him, turning water into blood and setting an entire nation on its ear.

These were the events and emotions that made worship his way of life, the defining moments that cemented his faith, secured his calling, and galvanized his will.

"He endured as seeing Him who is invisible."(Heb 11:27, NKJV)

And so even as the leader of millions – a man who was nearly worshiped himself by the tired, needy masses of Israelites – his genuine heart for worship prevented a power struggle between him and God. He never felt cramped by God's ideas and began thinking he could make it without His help. He had simply spent too much time with his head in the clouds, face down before God's awesome glory, to ever take credit for what the Lord was doing through him. Instead, you find him pleading with God from the wilderness in Exodus 33:15: *"If Your Presence does not go with us, do not bring us up from here." (NKJV)* As strong and respected a leader as Moses had become, nothing scared him more than making a move without God.

In fact, his unusual closeness to the Lord only deepened Moses' fear of Him. Yes, Moses and God were friends, but not buddies. You might think their close, one-on-one relationship would have developed in Moses a "me and God can take on all of you" attitude. But just like at the burning bush, he continued to come to God on his knees. He had experienced the impossible but he was still amazed. He had seen so much, but he never lost the wonder.

Finally, in The Song Of Moses (Deut 32), you see the man who had once said "I am slow of speech and slow of tongue" now captivating an entire nation with his tribute to God's power and goodness, charging the people to courage, and, despite being prevented from entering the Promised Land, worshiping with all his heart until the day God invited him atop Mount Nebo.

And brought him to an even greater place of worship.

Where Worship Begins
Babbie Mason

The act of divine worship
is the inestimable privilege
of man, the only created
being who bows
in humility and adoration.

~ Hosea Ballou

When we think of worship, it's easy to think of music. In our churches, the person who leads the singing is often called the worship pastor. We call the songs that they lead worship songs. Worship has been defined as a certain musical tempo, or style of songs containing a certain lyric. But according to the Bible, worship is not music at all. It is not a song. It is not a specific kind of lyric or melody. As a matter of fact, as important as music is, worship often happens without ever singing or playing a note.

In the Bible, the word worship means to prostrate oneself; to reverence and adore; to bow down or to stoop before the object of worship. Worship, then, must involve a humbling, a bowing down of one's heart and life before God. Worship must begin with a heart attitude that is right. It is that inner posture of humility and awe that leads to the outer expressions and demonstrations of worship. While singing is wonderful and lifting of the hands is a beautiful expression, I'm convinced that God is much more impressed with a heart that is right before Him.

If we are aware of God's presence, we can worship at any time. We are never out of His presence. He is always with us. He is constantly wooing us to draw near to Him. He pays attention when we call on Him. He delights in our efforts to communicate and commune with Him. God inhabits, He lives in or takes up residence in, our praise. Imagine that your heart is a house where God dwells. Picture Him pulling up an easy chair and making Himself at home in your worship.

It's not at all difficult to make this happen. When times are hard, express your undying devotion and your dependence on Him. When you arrive at your destination safely, thank Him. When you see a beautiful sunset or a star-filled night sky, take time to applaud Him. Tell Him you love Him. Ask for His guidance in your decision making. Cultivate an awareness of the presence of God. The words of Jeremiah 29:13 are so true: *"You will seek me and find me when you seek me with all your heart." (NIV)*

Worship becomes a joy when we focus on making worship an attitude, not an activity. It's a sad fact that many people think that worship is only confined to a designated place, or a set time of the day or week. Sometimes we even think we've done God a favor because we spend

- Where Worship Begins -
Babbie Mason

an hour in church once a week or set aside a few minutes of quiet time during the day. While this is good, it is not enough. When this is our way of thinking, when it is all we have to offer, worship becomes a religious ritual, a mere exercise.

True worshipers enjoy being in the presence of God at all times. We come to realize that it is not at all about what we can get from God, but being with Him. It is a conscious attitude that seeks to find ways to express love for God in our daily living. What is your driving passion? What is the one thing that keeps you up at night and consumes your thoughts during the day? Is it your work? Is it your money, or maybe your ministry? This is where your real attitude and your true motives will be revealed. Matthew 6:21 says, *"For wherever your treasure is, there your heart will be also." (NIV)*

A real hindrance to worship is how we view God. God is holy, sovereign, and has all authority. All of heaven and all of earth are in His control. It all belongs to Him. Instead of rising to God's standard of living, we have tried to reduce Him to ours. Instead of approaching Him with awe and respect, we often approach Him casually. We have lost sight of Him as Isaiah saw Him in Isaiah 6:1, *"Seated on his throne, high and lifted up and the train of his robe filled the temple." (NIV)* We don't see Him as a burning bush, as Moses saw Him. Moses' response was to take off his shoes, for he stood on holy ground. We must never forget that the God we worship has all wisdom and all power. He is worthy of all honor and glory. This is really where worship begins. It all starts with the recognition that God is holy and we are not.

God seeks those who will worship Him in spirit and in truth. Ask God to develop in you a keen sense and awareness of His presence. Approach Him with an attitude of humility and awe. Never forget that He is sovereign, holy, and has all authority.

Is it time to examine your heart and go back to where worship really begins? God is right there where you are. There is no better time to worship Him than right now.

Thirty Second Blessing

Kimberlee Stone

It is only when men
begin to worship that
they begin to grow.

~ Calvin Coolidge

Turning 30 was monumentally difficult for me. As a teenager, I envisioned the seasoned age of 29 to be the height of maturity, the age of all-knowing, the last year to do "it" if "it" was going to get done. My preconceived and pre-thirty ideas had already determined that by the time I reached that pinnacle of birthdays, my children would be marching off to kindergarten and I would be at the height of a successful career doing who knows what. After all, wouldn't it would be nearly impossible to leap tall buildings as middle age would be precariously hanging from my orthopedic shoe (you know the type I'm talking about...)? The dreams of my post-youth were so cliché that I hate to even write them: a good husband, three children, a big house with a large fenced in yard for the dog, and a hefty bank account with endless supplies of deposits that never needed balancing.

But what are you to do when your dream hits the cutting block like a knife coming to terms with an onion? Cry would be a good place to start. I cried because when I saw thirty candles on my birthday cake, the flames taunted me with the fact that most of my dreams were a complete bust. In truth, my idea of success wasn't brought on through godly prayer and seeking. I based success on what magazines and the media told me success looked like. What I *did* have, however, was a fantastic husband who loved God, a home in the form of a small condominium that sported a couple dozen wooden toothpicks for a fence, and a dog.

Yet to me, it all paled in comparison to there being no one to call me *Mom*. My prayer time was often riddled with anger, and my worship with tears. It all came down to the never ending question of "Why are you so angry with me, God?" I showed up at church and put on my best "everything's okay" face lest someone ask too many questions. "Why me?" I would say to myself like a whiny toddler. "Why can't I have what I want? And now?!" In a way, my desires became the focus of my worship; it was more about "I'm praising you Lord because of what I need. And I need children!"

Fast forward to ten years on the other side of 30. God has been good to give me the desires of my heart and so much more. Thirty years old is a blip in my mind that brings a grin to my face upon remembering it. This jaunt of nostalgia came to me last week when a friend stopped me at church; she had just celebrated her 30th birthday.

Like me, but for different reasons, she was not in the celebrating mood. I don't know her well enough to be privy to her hopes and dreams, but she is a single mom who works hard to make a good life for her eight year old daughter. I can imagine what she was wishing for as the candles, if only in her mind, fell silent to her huffing and puffing.

She had been at a shoe store until almost 9:00 on the evening of her birthday. The manager approached her in an effort to cheer her up or snap her out of whatever he sensed she was feeling. She told him it was her birthday, she was feeling a little blue, but to never fear, tomorrow would be better. She was drowning her well-deserved sorrow, for the moment, in the size 8 aisle of the black strappy sandal section.

Apparently struck by her, he made her a deal. He announced over the loud speaker that in honor of this special birthday girl, he was going to give her thirty seconds to pick out as many shoes as she could. If she dropped any, they would have to stay at the store. Otherwise they would be hers. At the sound of a make believe gun over the intercom, she grabbed whatever she could find in her size, unaware of what was even in most of the boxes as she fought to balance them in her arms. All in all, her thirty second shopping spree netted her 14 pairs of shoes for the low, low price of $5.00! Hearing her story, I squealed in delight. I couldn't think of anyone who deserved such a blessing more.

I am the first to admit that my worship has not always been for the right reason. Over the years, there have been many deep longings and desires that have clogged my way to God's heart. For me it was the need for a child and the disappointment of another year's unfulfilled hopes. For you, it may be a delayed healing for a sickness that you've prayed about for years, a broken marriage that has left you empty, or depression that hangs over you like a defining gray cloud.

Regardless, we have a choice to make in our worship. And if we find ourselves worshiping more because of a personal agenda that says, "If I worship, God will meet my needs," we miss out on God's blessings. True worship does not fluctuate like the candles on a birthday cake. It doesn't wane because we didn't get fourteen pairs of shoes for $5.00 or because our neighbor's house is bigger than ours.

We worship for a simple reason. We worship because of who God is. Forgiving, merciful, and omnipotent. Giving, gracious, and everlasting. The One who was, who is, and who is to come. The One who blesses us with life at each birthday, who cares enough to send blessings in the form of shoes.

That's just who He is!

The Responsibility of Worship
Mark Hodge

Whenever the method of worship becomes more important than the Person of worship, we have already prostituted our worship. There are entire congregations who worship praise and praise worship but who have not yet learned to worship God in Jesus Christ.

~ Judson Cornwall

In hopes of avoiding the ongoing worship war, the Church has begun to "agree to disagree" in our understanding and practice of worship. We have avoided bitter battles at the high cost of allowing everyone to define worship for themselves instead of following the instruction of scripture. This phenomenon has resulted in some popular but misguided new beliefs about our individual responsibility when we gather to worship with other believers.

1. Worship is between me and God. This belief allows the individual worshiper to decide what they are comfortable with in a worship gathering, especially in regard to how they express their worship (singing and praying out loud, raising hands in testimony, voicing affirmation and agreement, etc.). While we should be careful in questioning another's private worship, scripture challenges all of us with real responsibility when we gather with other believers. Private worship is just between me and God, but corporate worship carries a unique mandate to each other. Revelation 12:11 declares, *"They* (our brothers) *overcame him* (the accuser) *by the blood of the Lamb and by the word of their testimony." (NIV)* This affirms to us that the process of "overcoming" and finishing the race well includes declaring God's faithful work in our lives. You can stand in your prayer room and shout it loud, but the power of a testimony is in professing it to others. When we come to worship with our brothers, we obediently bring and share a testimony. As we share, God is honored and our brothers are encouraged. We even see our own faith strengthened as we declare the goodness and sovereignty of the Lord.

2. Corporate worship can be my private worship. There are those who do not practice a regular personal time of worship and come to a weekend church service expecting to catch up on their "God time." Unfortunately, corporate worship was never intended to be a substitute for private worship. Those who do not spend time in private worship have no sacrifice to bring to a weekend worship service. They cannot add their voice to the overwhelming song of the saints, nor truly understand the praise of those around them. It is in private worship that God instructs and speaks into your life. The abundance of that private time becomes the overflow of our church gatherings.

- The Responsibility of Worship -
Mark Hodge

3. Worship should be about what I like. This idea is better described as the weekend worship buffet. Worshipers sit back, survey the options, and choose the things they want to try. Some have even dubbed themselves critics, surveying food and service for others who will follow. To finish this analogy, worshipers focused on the buffet see only the menu items of a meal that hasn't been prepared for them! Worship is offered to the Lord and for His delight – not to us or for our benefit. God does bless and share with us as we gather to worship; *"Come near to God and he will come near to you." (Js 4:8, NIV)* But how dare we come to the table that has been set for Him, demanding to be served. When we come anticipating a particular musical performance or a moment that will make us feel good, we miss the point entirely – as well as the transforming presence of God.

4. Worship is about my needs. Some Christians arrive at a weekend worship time so focused on their personal need and circumstances that they are rendered powerless in the worship experience. In their depleted state, they resign themselves to allow others to do the worshiping for them. My wife, Cindy refers to this as "eating off of someone else's plate" in worship. Our personal circumstances can be very difficult, but they never incapacitate us to the sacrifice of worship. If we are breathing – and especially if our sins are under the blood of Jesus – we have the means and motivation to bring our worship before Him and the people, no matter what it costs us.

As we come to worship with other believers, it should be one big family reunion. We are grateful children, excited about the opportunity to thank the Father for His gifts, and determined to share stories with everyone in the family. And the table of worship, prepared for Him, is an overflowing table from which all of His children find lasting nourishment and strength.

Gideon

Lawrence Kimbrough

History remembers Gideon as a warrior. One of the best. One of the most strategically adept in all the Bible. But if you can silence for a moment the noise of blaring trumpets and crashing clay pots, you'll hear a different side to Gideon's story: that God sees more in people than they see in themselves, and that worship is His way of bringing it out.

You certainly don't get the feeling that there's fire in Gideon's belly the first time he shows up in scripture. Threshing wheat on the shadowy side of his daddy's winepress to avoid being spotted by the marauding Midianites, he's not the mental picture of a fearless fighting man in training. Yet an angel jolts him from his work, addressing him in terms almost as mysterious as this whole, unusual encounter: *"The LORD is with you, you mighty man of valor." (Jud 6:12, NKJV)*

Who, *ME*?

And in the process of conversation, Gideon revealed the one aspect of his nature that you'd think would disqualify him from appearing on God's short list of heroes.

Gideon was a skeptic.

Not the scoffing variety, but the kind who just needs to see it before he can believe it. The Thomas type. But you know what? God knew that all along. And in one of the most intriguing, endearing evidences of His love for mankind, God made room for Gideon's caution as He drew him into worship.

"Want me to wait here while you prepare an offering? Okay. Dew on the woolen fleece but not on the ground? All right. Oh, this time, dew on the ground, but keep the fleece dry? Yeah, I can do that for you, Gideon." God knew Gideon had to be brought along slowly.

In Gideon's first test of faith, dismantling the pagan altar in his father's backyard, God accepted his obedience even though he did it under cover of darkness, hoping to never be known as the culprit. And even after he winced through God's stringent selection process of assembling Israel's army, paring 32,000 down to 300 to make his conquering army less suspicious, God graciously gave him something tangible to hold on to:

"Arise, go down against the camp, for I have delivered it into your hand. But if you are afraid to go down, go down to the camp with

Purah your servant, and you shall hear what they say; and afterward your hands shall be strengthened to go down against the camp." (Jud 7:9-11, NKJV)

And down among the nighttime fires of the Midianite tents, in one of those reflective moments when brave men confess their honest fears, Gideon overheard something unbelievable. Members of the world's mightiest military were scared to death of the God who ruled Israel – and of its leader in battle. A man named...

Gideon.

Watch his eyes widen, coming close to giving himself away. See him motion abruptly to his servant, declaring their spy mission completed. See him reach a point beyond earshot of the Midianite encampment, where he can clench his fists in triumph and his teeth in a victorious "Yessssss!" The Bible simply says that, on hearing the enemy's confession, "he worshiped."

You can bet it was a lot more than that.

His fear was gone. His skepticism vanquished. His courage invincible. "The sword of the LORD and of Gideon!"

And the rest is history.

What's Mine Is Mine
Gordon Mularski

Make sure you don't take
things for granted and go
slack in working for the
common good; share what you
have with others. God takes
particular pleasure in acts
of worship — a different
kind of "sacrifice" — that
take place in the kitchen
and workplace and
on the streets.

~ Paul

Imagine that you arrive at the church early. The sound of laughter and fellowship is absent from the foyer. There is no usher there to greet you. No bulletin handed to you as you enter the sanctuary. You feel kind of hollow inside. It is foreign for you to be in the "House of the Lord" without all the business and festive commotion usually associated with your worship routine. You quietly find a seat and begin to scan the room once more.

In the silence of the moment you sense that someone is there but you can't see her. You feel as if you are sharing a moment with someone and you don't know who. Then you hear something. It is faint at first. You can't identify it as conversation or crying. Finally you realize that behind you there is a woman sitting in the last row. She has found a seat tucked back in the furthest corner of the church. She is obviously emotionally engaged in the moment.

You don't know how to respond as you hear her pray in a voice almost too closed to get the words out. "If you will give me a son, I will give him back to you." You feel for her but dismiss her as another sad story of a woman unable to have children. Thankfully, about that time the pastor comes in and you don't have to worry about how to comfort the broken hearted woman.

The pastor makes his way down the aisle and begins to talk with her. You can't hear what he is saying but it appears that the Lord has given this man the wisdom of Solomon. The woman's face lights up. They pray and it seems like the weight of the world has been lifted off her shoulders.

A couple of years have passed and you have given little thought to the incident when suddenly you are brought back. You're sitting in your usual seat and the pastor informs the crowd that it is time to dedicate a child to the Lord. You get ready to watch the pastor wrestle with a kid who does not want to be held. It's always a train wreck when he tries to bless these children.

It hits you when you see the woman. That's her, that's the broken woman you saw a couple of years back. Man, did God ever come through on that one! The pastor shares the story you saw unfold first hand. The crowd goes wild and God is given the praise. "That's the kind of God I serve," is what keeps going through your mind.

Then, after the celebration and prayer of blessing, the service takes a very strange twist. The woman whispers something in the ear of the pastor and he grants her an opportunity to share with the church. Her voice cracks as she gives God the praise for her son. Everyone is as moved as she is. "I asked Him to bless me with a son and He did," she said. "But when I asked Him to bless me with a son, I also made a promise. I promised that if He would give me a son that I would give him back."

At this point, she breaks down and the pastor does his best to comfort her. You can feel her range of emotions; you have become part of her story. After she gains her composure she steps back to the microphone and says something you will never forget. "I am here today to honor my promise to the Lord." She looks at the pastor and says, "I am giving him back to the Lord. I want you to raise him." She then kisses the child and hands him over to the pastor. She walks down off the stage and right out the back entrance.

The story you just visited is a 21st century version of the story of Hannah and her son Samuel. When we put it in today's terms, the level of sacrifice is somewhat realized. Her story identifies one of the attributes of a true worshiper. A true worshiper gives whatever is required. A true worshiper's gift to God will have cost something. A true worshiper never holds on to what belongs to the Lord. To sum it all up, a true worshiper is a giver.

I wonder if our measure of worship has been tied to our emotional expression for too long. What would happen with our lives' "possessions" if they were truly viewed as our gifts from Him to be given to Him? What would happen in our churches if our service was truly dedicated to Him?

It might be time to express our worship in the real material world instead of the emotional expression that oftentimes costs us very little.

Repairing the Altar
Patrick Tharp

A person will worship
something, have no doubt
about that. We may
think our tribute is paid
in secret in the dark
recesses of our hearts,
but it will out. That which
dominates our imaginations
and our thoughts will
determine our lives,
and our character.
Therefore, it behooves
us to be careful what
we worship, for what we
are worshiping we are
becoming.

~ Ralph Waldo Emerson

Have you ever read a scripture and just gotten stopped in your tracks? I sure have. While reading the account of the prophet Elijah in 1 Kings, I came across an amazing section of scripture with which we are all probably very familiar.

The children of Israel had been delivered from Egypt and had been given the law from the Lord, chronicled in the books of Leviticus, Numbers, and Deuteronomy. The mighty servant of the Lord, Joshua, was raised up to take Israel into the land that the Lord had promised them.

We then come to the book of Judges which tells the sad story of the children of Israel following after idolatry, forsaking the Lord in their hearts and actions, repenting, getting delivered, and repeating this cycle again and again. The Lord had warned His people many times through His prophets and servants not to forsake the way of the Lord.

Now we come to 1 Kings, where we join Elijah on Mt. Carmel for his showdown with the prophets of Baal (we all know whose God shows up!). The altar of the Lord, the place of fellowship and communion where the people came before the Lord and the Lord met with the people, had been broken down.

"Then Elijah said to all the people, 'Come near to me.' So all the people came near to him. And he repaired the altar of the Lord that was broken down." (1 Kgs 18:30, NKJV)

In many situations it was out and out sinful rebellion that caused their altars to be broken and torn down. Light cannot have fellowship with darkness. One cannot fellowship with the Lord when sin stands between you. But an equally grievous sin is the sin of neglect. The altar in Elijah's day had been neglected. It was broken down from not being used. It fell apart while the high places and groves, where other gods were worshiped, were well kept and flourished.

Today under the new covenant, we don't need to build a fire and offer up the blood of a bull or lamb on an altar to meet God. The Lamb of God who takes away the sins of the world has paid our price! Our hearts have now become the altar. Our bodies are now the temples. How sad when the altar in our lives is neglected and becomes broken down, that place where we spend time alone with our heavenly Father.

But altars of fellowship and intimacy can be restored. Jesus told the church in Ephesus to remember, repent, and return (Rev 2:1-5). Repeating those basic disciplines of daily obedience, prayer, fellowship, and being daily in the Bible is the right track toward rebuilding the altar in our lives. The "fire of the Lord" wants to blaze afresh in our hearts today, if we would only prepare the altar! Matthew Henry said, *"If we, in sincerity, offer our hearts to God, He will, by His grace, kindle a holy fire in them."*

We all know how much time we have in a day, what we need to get done, where we need to go. But we must not sacrifice intimacy and communion with our Lord to all the stuff that fights for our time and attention.

Let's all take inventory today. Has the altar of intimacy and fellowship become broken down through neglect? Have the stones of God's word fallen to the ground while other monuments in our lives stand tall and strong? Have our hearts become the "sacred space" for something other than meeting with God?

The Anointing

Dr. David C. Cooper

What you are is God's gift to you; what you do with yourself is your gift to God.

~ Danish Proverb

Today we hear a lot about anointing. But what does it mean? The Hebrew word for anointing is "masha." It appears 70 times in the Old Testament and means "to smear," "to rub," or "consecrate." To consecrate means "to dedicate," "to devote," and "to set apart for God's purpose." The Greek words for anointing are "chrio" (verb) and "charisma" (noun) from which we get the word charismatic or gifts of the Spirit.

The anointing is embodied in the role of the shepherd and the sheep. Sheep are often wounded in the process of traveling and grazing. Cuts to the head or nose happen while grazing among thorns. Sheep get tired from the heat of the day and the long treks across slopes and plains. The shepherd's oil was used to bind up the wounds of the sheep.

There is another interesting use of oil or ointment. During the summer, swarms of insects and parasites disturb the sheep. Especially troublesome, according to Philip Keller in *A Shepherd Looks at Psalm 23*, are the nose flies. They get into the nasal cavity and lay eggs which causes severe inflammation in the sheep's head. Shepherds will apply the ointment in advance to protect the sheep from such parasites. A shepherd will also smear the heads of the rams with oil so that when they become combative they will slip off each other if they butt heads to keep them from injury.

The oil represents the Holy Spirit's healing ministry. The anointing work of the shepherd is an ongoing experience just as the Holy Spirit continues this work of empowerment for service and healing for our spiritual wounds. God gives "the oil of gladness" for times of depression and discouragement (Is 61:3).

The oil also represents consecration for service (see Ex 29:7; 1 Sam 16:13). In Hebrew culture there were three anointed offices of service which typified the Messiah: prophet, priest, and king. All three were anointed in a ceremony that involved pouring oil made from olives on them, which symbolized the presence and power of the Spirit. The title Messiah (Hebrew) or Christ (Greek) means the "Anointed One." Jesus is the Anointed One: prophet, priest, *and* king. Christians have received an anointing from Jesus Himself. The anointing, then, is the presence and power of the Holy Spirit in our lives. So the word Christian can be taken to mean one who is anointed.

To be anointed means to be dedicated and consecrated to God, to be empowered to do the work of God and to live as anointed servants of the Lord. Are all Christians anointed by the Holy Spirit? Absolutely!

> "But you have an anointing from the Holy One (Jesus), and all of you know the truth...the anointing you received from him remains in you." (1 Jn 2:20, 27, NIV)

While we are indeed anointed, the fact remains that we can either be open or closed to the anointing. We can allow the anointing to work in our lives or hinder it. We can be channels of His anointing to others or keep it within ourselves.

David

Lawrence Kimbrough

If worship had a name, it would be David.

Like a puppy let out after being shut up in the garage all day, worship just crawled all over him. It darted up his sleeves, ran down his backbone, spun around his waist, and nipped at his heels.

Worshiping the Lord was his passion. To breathe was to praise. To live was to worship.

So when you read about David in the Bible, you pick up more than facts and dates, battle plans and court records, Bathshebas and Goliaths. You see inside a man's heart – a man after God's own heart.

Born the littlest brother into the most ordinary of families, he grew up catching the leftovers from the older boys' chores and duties. Tending sheep was boring, thankless work. But David was able to look into the grim face of tedium and see the approving smile of God – the simple pleasures of being able "to lie down in green pastures," of being led "beside the still waters" by an unseen, all-seeing Guide (Ps 23:2).

Surely it was out there under an early evening sky, or during the first, methodical paces of another scorching day, that the kid who would one day sing his songs for an entire nation would practice on an audience of disinterested sheep, their blank stares receiving his hearty laugh and a playful slap on the ribs.

That was just who he was. Free. Energetic. Uninhibited.

Remember the day he led the exuberant processional that accompanied the Ark of the Covenant back to Jerusalem? There he was, dancing like a crazy man, too wound up in worship to care that his wife was watching the whole thing from the palace balcony, rolling her eyes at his revelry. Shoot, David didn't care. *"I'll be even more undignified than this,"* he said, *"and will be humble in my own sight"* if kingly etiquette keeps me from celebrating the goodness of God (2 Sam 6:22, NKJV).

See, something deep had occurred back in his boyhood. Something that had turned this naturally expressive young man into a compelling leader and inexhaustible poet. Long before Bethlehem would be known as the City of David, even longer before a God-man named Jesus would cut miraculously into his royal bloodline, the sands of that ancient village were dotted with the thick drops of God's anointing oil, streaming off the ruddy chin of a shepherd boy handpicked for greatness.

"The Spirit of the LORD came upon David from that day forward."
(1 Sam 16:13, NKJV)

"From that day forward" would encompass victories and events that were the dreams of every Hebrew boy, as well as failures and crises that remain the worst nightmares of every husband and father.

But every experience – no matter how crushing, no matter how ecstatic – would bring a lyric to his lips.

That's because David's worship was more than praise, more steady and dependable than emotion. Worship was his life, and nothing about him could avoid being swept up in it, whether it came out as angelic elation or gut-level despair. He poured as much awe and honesty into saying "I will sing to the LORD as long as I live" as in crying "How long, O Lord? Will you forget me forever?"

Everything went up to God – *everything* – even when he felt the disappointment of being passed over as (you'd think) the logical builder of the temple, Israel's first permanent house of worship. But in his voice, you hear a humble man who was…well, who was okay with surrendering his human ambitions into God's eternal purposes. *"Who am I, O LORD God? And what is my house, that you have brought me this far?" (2 Sam 7:18, NKJV)* I don't deserve what you've done for me already, Lord. I just pray that *"Your name be magnified forever." (2 Sam 7:26, NKJV)*

And though the temple building would eventually fall to the torches of the enemy, anyway, and be lost to future generations, David would lead God's people in worship for all time.

Even today, we find him leading us.

Tears of Joy
Harlan Rogers

I never knew how to
worship until I knew
how to love.

~ Henry Ward Beecher

I used to wonder: *how do I really praise God?*

I would read the Psalms where we are exhorted to praise Him and to rejoice and be glad. Yet so many times I felt that to do so was more of a perfunctory exercise of obedience rather than a true expression of my heart. I would go to a church service where scriptures like "enter His gates with thanksgiving and His courts with praise" would be read, yet in the environment of that gathering, we all seemed rather quiet, unresponsive, and almost as though the exhortations to praise Him were falling on deaf ears. In my case, I now know it was because I had not yet learned what true gratitude toward God really was.

Our faith in God is to "usher us in" to His presence. It unlocks the doorway to entering into a true parent-child relationship. This personal relationship with God is on a much higher plane than our natural, earthly relationships with our earthly parents. We have a relationship with One who is perfect in love toward us, One who never fails, One on whom we can always rely, and in whom we can trust without fear and without question. This kind of faithfulness is rarely experienced in this life. No wonder it takes time and understanding for our minds to begin to grasp the depth of God's love toward us.

"Herein is love, not that we loved God, but that he loved us, and sent his Son to be the propitiation for our sins. Beloved, if God so loved us, we ought also to love one another. No man hath seen God at any time. If we love one another, God dwelleth in us, and his love is perfected in us. Hereby know we that we dwell in him, and he in us, because he hath given us of his Spirit. And we have seen and do testify that the Father sent the Son to be the Saviour of the world. Whosoever shall confess that Jesus is the Son of God, God dwelleth in him, and he in God. And we have known and believed the love that God hath to us. God is love; and he that dwelleth in love dwelleth in God, and God in him. Herein is our love made perfect, that we may have boldness in the day of judgment: because as he is, so are we in this world. There is no fear in love; but perfect love casteth out fear: because fear hath *torment. He that feareth is not made perfect in love. We love Him because He first loved us." (1 Jn 4:10-19, KJV)*

This is the reality of the nature of our relationship with God. This is the creative spark that elicits true gratitude in the hearts of those who believe. The more that we truly understand all that God has done for us and the depth of His wonderful love toward us, the more that praise and gratitude simply flow from our hearts and lives toward Him.

I would liken it to how natural a laugh is when we experience something truly funny. It is a natural response that just happens. We do not have to try to praise God or to worship Him. When the deep realization of God's mercy and goodness toward us is really understood, our love and praise and worship of God will be as natural as our love for our own children. It's just there, and it is always there.

Our God is a wonderful God. The heart that truly recognizes His love, His mercies, His forgiveness, and His truth will be filled with genuine praise and thanks and adoration. We will not have to attempt to manufacture a ritualistic expression. True gratitude and thankfulness will stir our hearts so that we can do nothing other than worship Him in truth.

This is the nature of a loving relationship. True love expresses itself. Love is an active force. True worship will flow naturally toward our heavenly Father as we truly understand and know the depth of His love for us. I will also say that it is this love, from Him and for Him, that is the motivating force which causes us to desire to be obedient to Him in our lives.

God is good. He is merciful and kind. His love for us knows no bounds.

Communion

Drew Cline

I've always wanted
to go to church and
sing one song,
then for the rest of
our worship time,
just go and love on
each other.

~ Michael W. Smith

I love learning about history – going to places built by our forefathers, or watching Discovery Channel shows about wars or inventions from long ago. The specifics don't really matter to me. I just love seeing where we've come from and trying to imagine what it must have been like back in that time, whenever it was.

My wife and I live in Franklin, TN and there's a lot of Civil War history here. Around every corner is an antique shop with Civil War era relics and treasures. I love seeing old remnants of the soldier's uniforms and weapons. I stare and wonder what that soldier was like, what life must have been for him. There's just something interesting to me about the fact that others have gone before us, to fight for our freedom, to build a great nation, or to raise the family from which I can trace my heritage.

Recently my wife and I were with my 93-year-old grandmother looking through her pictures, complete with horse and buggy and frowning ancestors (I've always wondered why turn-of-the-century folks didn't smile much). As I looked through these old pictures I couldn't help asking myself, "What in the world do I have in common with these people?" My only reasonable answer was blood. They're my relatives. These were my people. As I began to think of them as family, they didn't just look like people in an old photo anymore. I found myself wondering about their lives, their families, their faith.

Sometimes I think believers need to remember that others have gone before us. We're not reinventing the wheel here. Amazing, passionate men and women have led the way for us so that we could be who we are today as the church. Why is it that we so rarely think of them? My guess is that we're too busy with tomorrow to think about yesterday but it's an important thing to do.

There are a lot of ways to draw from and remember the past. We can sing hymns and tell the stories of the amazing, colorful writers who gave us such melodic theology and beautiful music. We can read their biographies or examine their artwork. But my favorite way to remember those who've gone before is by taking communion. When we read those words of Jesus saying "Do this in remembrance of me," I begin to try and wrap my brain around all those followers of His who read that same

- Communion -
Drew Cline

scripture and then obeyed by observing the elements. Think of all the styles of churches, both in faith and construction, as well as generation after generation of believers following this commandment. I'm sure it looked quite different from one country to the next, different languages and methods, but all with the desire to be obedient and follow His example in remembering.

"Communion" speaks of two different types of remembering. One is personal – thinking of how the Lord has redeemed you and given you grace and mercy, that in His goodness you recognize that He has forgiven you and given you life. But the Bible also uses words and phrases like "we" and "together." Many of those scriptures are talking about our collective remembrance of Jesus and the price He paid for His church.

For me, it helps to know that I'm not alone in this journey. My community is not the first one to struggle with issues of faith and living for Jesus; I'm joined by a cloud of believers around the world dating back to Passover, up to the Last Supper, continuing all the way to today and well into tomorrow. It reminds me that I'm stronger for being a part of this family of faith, blessed to continue the journey that so many have started before me. As I look around the sanctuary, I am reminded that Jesus and His death as well as the faith of our fathers are what we all have in common. The blood.

I encourage you to gather your worship team, your wife and children, your small group, and take communion truly as a family. You won't believe the difference it will make in your worship. Worship was meant to be offered in community and communion is meant to be a fabulous expression of it. Don't just rush through. Allow the power of the Holy Spirit to cleanse and convict you, to bring to your minds the very real and transforming moments of Jesus' grace over us. You might want to incorporate a hymn to help drive home the practice of remembrance. Encourage each other, and remember that you're not alone but are carrying on a tradition of faith that is thousands of years old.

Holy Is Your Name
David M. Edwards

All of history is moving toward one great goal, the white-hot worship of God and his Son among all the peoples of the earth. Missions exists because worship doesn't. Worship is ultimate, not missions, because God is ultimate, not man....

When this age is over, and the countless millions of the redeemed fall on their faces before the throne of God, missions will be no more. It is a temporary necessity.

But worship abides forever.

~ John Piper

In the summer of 2003 I was beginning to write for a Psalms project with Margaret Becker. We were digging through the Psalms and looking for specific ones that we felt drawn to for consideration for the album. As a songwriter and as a believer, like many others, I had always found comfort, solace, and healing in the Psalms – specifically in the words of King David. The Psalms are the most underlined book in my Bible.

With that thought in mind, I have always approached the worship of the Holy with awe, fear, and trembling. He is not an idol, statue, charm, or bumper sticker. He is Almighty God, Jehovah, Creator of all that is. The sight of the omission of vowels in "G_d's" name in the Tanakh (Jewish scripture) has always served as a reminder to me in a very practical way that His Name is so holy, that even when we spell it we should use caution.

We live in a world that, for the most part, does not respect God or His great Name. Thus, it behooves us to honor that Name in our worship, the way we live, and by what comes out of our mouths. To this day, when people take God's Name in vain, or I hear the proverbial exclamation, "Oh my __," I cringe. One of the Ten Commandments is that we should not take His Name in vain. When His Name has become nothing more than a tagline for every time we're surprised at the price of gas, something is wrong!

These meanderings are kind of where my heart was one morning when I sat down at the piano to worship the Lord by myself. I saw the words that I was bringing to Him as almost tangible gifts to give to Him to express my deep appreciation for all that He had done for me. Just like one of my kids who still gets a thrill out of asking me to "Close your eyes and hold out your hands, Dad" when they want to give me a present, that is exactly how I felt that morning when these words came to me. I had something to give to Him – an offering of love.

The chorus was the gift I presented: *"Holy is Your Name, Holy is Your Name, Holy is Your Name, Holy is Your Name."* That's it – no other words were needed for my present. In the bridge I extolled other names by which He has revealed Himself to us, *"Mighty God, Redeemer, Lord, Friend, Emmanuel,"* etc. but then returned to the anthem, *"Holy is Your*

Name!"

We may not all be songwriters or worship leaders, but all of us should bring Him gifts! All of us should present our highest praise and deepest worship to Him who alone is worthy of glory and honor. Hebrews 13:15 says, *"Therefore by Him let us continually offer the sacrifice of praise to God, that is, the fruit of our lips, giving thanks to His name." (NKJV)* It does say "continually," and it does say, "the fruit of our lips." Each of us should bring a gift that He can open and enjoy.

Angels were created to serve God and praise Him continually. I am sure that He enjoys the singing of angels – which John said in Revelation sounded like many waterfalls – but oh the joy that must swell in the Lord's heart every time one of His kids approach Him and says, "Close Your eyes and hold Your hands out; I brought You something!"

Solomon

Lawrence Kimbrough

Solomon is best remembered for his wisdom, but above all, he was an extravagant worshiper.

Raised in the home of his father King David, he rarely knew a day when the angelic strum of the lyre or the exuberance of a morning praise psalm didn't hum through the palace. And surely, he must have been close to his father and embraced the heart of his worshipful ministry, for after the king's death, Solomon immediately began fulfilling the unfinished business of David's noble but bloody reign – the building of the temple, the resting place for the Ark of the Covenant.

He envisioned it as a place where worshipers would *"burn before Him sweet incense, for the continual shewbread, for the burnt offerings morning and evening, on the Sabbaths, on the New Moons, and on the set feasts of the LORD our God. This is an ordinance forever to Israel." (2 Chr 2:4, NKJV)*

And he spared no expense. His dad had left him nearly 500 tons of gold and silver to decorate the walls and to fashion the furnishings. Except for gathering some lumber and a few other building materials here and there, what else did he think he needed?

But Solomon had also received his father's heart as an inheritance, a heart that smothered under its own inadequacy of putting its worshipful feelings into thoughts, thoughts into words, words into music, music into loyalty and devotion.

Twenty-four hours weren't enough. Week-long ceremonies weren't enough. Mountains of animal offerings weren't enough. The sheer inexpressibility of his thanks and wonder for Almighty God left him panting to say more, to do more, to love more – to *be* more.

His prayer at the dedication ceremony (recorded in 1 Kings, chapter 8) pours from a heart born to worship, a man who understood that his lavish wealth couldn't buy God's mercy, that his knowledge couldn't persuade God's favor. Solomon knew full well that God didn't need Solomon's temple. *"Behold, heaven and the heaven of heavens cannot contain You. How much less this temple which I have built!" (1 Kgs 8:27, NKJV)* But he knew that he and the people desperately needed God – the keeper of the covenant, the fountain of forgiveness, the teacher of all truth – the God who rode the heavens, yet chose to humble Himself and hear the prayers of His children down here on earth.

Still, if not maintained, the heart can slowly build up a taste for its own pleasures.

And when the LORD'S house takes seven years to build but your own house takes 13, when the entire temple could sit inside one room in your new palace, when the fawn-eyed requests of 1,000 or more foreign wives wear down the gears on your discernment, you're likely to justify anything. Like building hilltop shrines so your pagan-worshiping wives won't have to travel so far to offer sacrifice to their gods. Like levying higher and higher taxes to feed your lust for luxury.

These are the sad footnotes to Solomon's story. The lasting images he leaves us in the pages of Ecclesiastes are the sour ramblings of a bitter old man. *"I looked on all the works that my hands had done and on the labor in which I had toiled; and indeed all was vanity and grasping for the wind. There was no profit under the sun,"* he would write (Ecc 2:11, NKJV), failing to realize that worshiping God is its own reward. Catching a glimpse of God's glory and discovering His steadfast love through every situation are the life supports from another world that keep you truly alive in this one.

And in his parting shot, though it's filtered through the pain of someone who chose to learn it the hard way, he spoke the truth he knew as a boy but lost as a man. *"Fear God and keep His commandments, for this is man's all."* *(Ecc 12:13, NKJV)*

He died a much-too-young 60, yet he had actually died many years before, when his heart had stopped beating for the one true God.

Yielded Instruments

Patrick Tharp

An authentic life is
the most personal
form of worship.

~ Sarah Ban Breathnach

Do not let any part of your body become an instrument of evil to serve sin. Instead, give yourselves completely to God, for you were dead, but now you have new life. So use your whole body as an instrument to do what is right for the glory of God.

~ Romans 6:13, NLT

I've never seen a guitar or drum set, sitting alone and unattended, all of a sudden yield music. Instruments only work when they are under the control of a musician. They yield to the hands of the one holding them. As a musician I love the music, beats, and grooves. I'm drawn to the entire experience of magnifying the Lord in music and song. It is a glorious interchange from our hearts to His.

Jesus said that the Father seeks those who worship Him in spirit and in truth. I know that true worship is much deeper than a song structure, a drum beat, or a chord progression. As Jesus spoke to the woman at the well in John 4, notice she didn't have a guitar or microphone in her hand. She wasn't a musician but she was a lost and broken soul who needed to drink from the living waters that flow from Jesus. She was religious but not righteous. She knew where she went to worship but not who she worshiped. Her heart was not in tune with her Creator.

True worship is always a matter of the heart. The heart is the instrument that each of us brings to the Lord for any act of service. Out of the heart will flow that with which we have filled it. That's why we are urged to *"keep thy heart with all diligence; for out of it are the issues of life." (Prov 4:23, KJV)* Every act of service should be our opportunity to worship.

A true worshiper is a yielded disciple of Jesus. Daniel chapter 3 gives us an awesome insight into this. Three young men chose not to yield to the worship of the world, and chose to instead yield in worship to their God. As the people heard the music, they were to fall and worship this image of gold, which King Nebuchadnezzar had set up. Whoever did not fall and worship was to be cast into the fiery furnace. Everyone bowed but three young Jewish men: Shadrach, Meshach, and Abednego. The king gave them a second chance to compromise, but they refused.

- Yielded Instruments -

Patrick Tharp

"If it be so, our God whom we serve is able to deliver us from the burning fiery furnace, and he will deliver us out of thine hand, O king. But if not, be it known unto thee, O king, that we will not serve thy gods, nor worship the golden image which thou hast set up." (Dan 3:17-18, KJV)

These guys had determined long before the trial that they only served and worshiped the true and living God. There was no room for compromise, no matter what the outcome was. The king in his fury bound them and cast them into the fiery furnace, which was so hot that it killed the men who threw them in. But their God stood with them and brought about a great deliverance. King Nebuchadnezzar responded with great praise:

"Blessed be the God of Shadrach, Meshach, and Abednego, who hath sent his angel, and delivered his servants that trusted in him, and have changed the king's word, and yielded their bodies, that they might not serve nor worship any god, except their own God." (Dan 3:28, KJV)

This worship service had no musical instruments, song sheets, or sound gear, but these three men brought a pleasing offering to their God: yielded obedience.

Can you imagine if my guitar wanted to play the songs it wanted to, instead of the ones I wanted it to play? We would have war! Yet that is what happens in the life of a believer who yields to the world or the flesh instead of Jesus. An inner war breaks out. You can have all the outward trappings of worship and yet not be yielded. This is the "vain worship" Jesus warned us about. Rather than be caught in that war, *"give your bodies to God because of all he has done for you. Let them be a living and holy sacrifice – the kind he will find acceptable. This is truly the way to worship him." (Rom 12:1, NLT)*

So today we bring an instrument to the Lord: your heart, my heart. Let's let the Master tune it and use it for His glory. Let His songs flow, let our will go, and fruit will grow.

Room 313

Greg Long

It is in the process of being worshiped that God communicates His presence to men.

~ C.S. Lewis

It was my junior year in college and I was on Thanksgiving break. I had been traveling and singing all three years with college groups. Financial aid was helping me pay for college and I supplemented this by working for the school as a singer.

As I sat on my friend's couch watching MTV, I became more and more depressed. I was watching rock stars sing and saw people falling at their feet almost worshiping them. All the money in the world seemed to be theirs as they became famous beyond their wildest dreams – not to speak of all the beautiful women happy to "keep their company." I began wondering if traveling and singing for Jesus was the right decision. There was no fame, money was tight. Instead of private jets I travelled in maxi vans pulling trailers. And that was on the good days!

About a month later I was sitting in room 313, my dorm room at Trinity Bible College, and opened the Bible to Psalm 73. I began to read about Asaph. He seemed to know exactly what I was talking about. He was envying the rich and famous, as it were.

"But as for me, my feet had almost slipped; I had nearly lost my foothold. For I envied the arrogant when I saw the prosperity of the wicked. They have no struggles; their bodies are healthy and strong. They are free from the burdens common to man; they are not plagued by human ills. Therefore pride is their necklace; they clothe themselves with violence... Their mouths lay claim to heaven, and their tongues take possession of the earth. Therefore their people turn to them and drink up waters in abundance... This is what the wicked are like: always carefree, they increase in wealth." (NIV)

Suddenly I realized God was speaking to me. Maybe Asaph had been watching MTV as well. He saw what I saw and it was dragging his spirit down as well. Then he said what I felt like saying:

"Surely in vain have I kept my heart pure; in vain have I washed my hands in innocence. All day long I had been plagued; I have been punished every morning... When I tried to understand

all this, it was oppressive to me. Till I entered the sanctuary of God." (NIV)

"Till I entered the sanctuary"... Dorm room 313 Kessler Hall in Ellendale, North Dakota quickly became the sanctuary of God. My eyes were opened, my heart suddenly turned from bitterness to gratefulness. Being in the presence of God, the sanctuary, made all the difference in the world. I continued to read to the end of the chapter and saw my ending alongside of Asaph's.

"When my heart was grieved and my spirit embittered, I was senseless and ignorant; I was a brute beast before you. Yet I am always with you; You hold me by my right hand. You guide me with your counsel, and afterward you will take me into glory. Whom have I in heaven but you? And earth has nothing I desire beside you. My flesh and my heart may fail, but God is the strength of my heart and my portion forever. Those who are far from you will perish; you destroy all who are unfaithful to you. But as for me, it is good to be near God. I have made the Sovereign LORD my refuge; I will tell of all your deeds." (NIV)

Where are you as you read this? In a hotel room? Your office at the church? Your living room at home? Wherever you are, make it the sanctuary of God, a place where He is welcome and sought after.

A Perfect Heart
Reba Rambo-McGuire

When I worship, I would rather my heart be without words than my words be without heart.

~ Lamar Boschman

What is it about rivers?

There are songs hiding in the murky deep and lapping their rhythms on the gurgling shore. Night winds and katydids hum their ancient melodies to listening hearts.

My husband Dony and I have learned a few river secrets. Many years ago we rented a cozy houseboat and managed to dock it in a secluded cove of our favorite river. For two days and nights we worshiped and wrote, listened and labored, and crafted six new songs. The third morning Dony was up before sunrise determined to catch a big catfish for our farewell breakfast. I, being a great woman of faith, was inside rustling up bacon and eggs. I glanced out the tiny kitchen window, admiring the swirling mist on the sunrise waters. Then I saw him.

Some people get a look when they come down with a cold. Dony gets a look when he comes down with a song.

I quickly turned off the burners, grabbed a pen and paper, and rushed over to the waiting keyboard and tape recorder. Dony walked in, sat down, and started playing and singing:

Morning sun light of creation
I continued...
Grassy fields a velvet floor
We alternated lines...
Silver clouds a shimmering curtain
He's designed a perfect world
I'm amazed at His talents
Stand in awe of One so great
Now my soul begins to sing out
To the Source from which it came

Bless the Lord Who reigns in beauty
Bless the Lord Who reigns with wisdom and with power
Bless the Lord Who reigns my life with so much love
He can make a perfect heart!

- A Perfect Heart -
Reba Rambo-McGuire

In moments the effortless song "A Perfect Heart" was born. It was as if God was saying, "You've been out here worshiping and working; now this one is on Me!"

Right after its inception, the head of the label we were recording for asked if he could have the first demo of the song. "My brother is scheduled for a heart transplant…there's not a lot of hope. Maybe God could use this song to build his faith."

The next few weeks his brother listened to "A Perfect Heart" several times a day until he began to know that God was healing him. When a donor was found and the surgery was finally scheduled, the surgeons were dumbfounded. They discovered another Surgeon had been there before them! The primary care physician walked into the hospital family waiting room shaking his head with tears in his eyes. "We can't explain it! We know his medical history; I personally saw the 'before and after' tests," he said. "All the challenges that were there just aren't there anymore. He has the heart of a young healthy man. This man has a perfect heart."

What is it about a song?

A song has the uncanny ability to heal or debilitate, teach or pervert, motivate or depress. It can stir love or lust, worship or war, faith or fear.

A song can set an atmosphere of hope and expectancy that can activate the very Word of God in the heart of the listener.

David experienced the power of an anointed song. When he ministered before the Lord with a perfect heart, the evil spirits that tormented Saul departed.

When Paul and Silas were in jail and began to sing songs at midnight, there was an earthquake that shook all the prison doors open and wells of salvation came bubbling forth.

Are we worshiping the Father at our darkest hour with clean hands and perfect hearts? Are we writing and singing songs with that kind of earthshaking presence? Are we listening for His whisperings in the night breeze? Are we mining all the mysteries in the Deep? Are we thirsty enough to run to the Water?

Maybe it's time we all go to the river.

"A Perfect Heart" was written by Dony and Reba Rambo-McGuire, Oohs and Ahs, Mak-a-nu-me, and Lexicon Music, ASCAP

Elijah

Lawrence Kimbrough

Elijah was Israel's most fiery prophet. He was John the Baptist before John the Baptist was – a woodsy renegade who could tighten his leather belt, march into uninvited places with an unwelcome, unpopular message, and stir up the ire of important people.

And like John, he was living proof that when a person takes seriously his calling and relationship with God, there's going to be trouble. Trouble fitting in. Trouble from people who take offense or who don't understand. Sometimes, even trouble avoiding the temptation to give up. Elijah experienced all of these. And more.

But the trouble cut both ways. To a nation as infatuated with sin and pleasure as it was infuriated by God's intrusive law and old-fashioned demands, Elijah became the *"troubler of Israel." (1 Kgs 18:17, NKJV)* His desperate, anguished cry pierced the darkest nights of Israel's history, pleading, *"How long will you falter between two opinions? If the LORD is God, follow Him; but if Baal, follow him." (1 Kgs 18:21, NKJV)*

Quit pretending to be one thing and doing another!

Yet his appeal was generally greeted by deaf ears and rolling eyes. That's the sometimes lonely walk of a worshiper. And Elijah knew it well, enduring the scorn, threats, and alienation of standing practically alone for God, even in the midst of God's covenant people.

There was even a time soon after his monumental clash with the prophets of Baal on Mt. Carmel that the Bible caught up with him a day's walk deep into the wilderness, where he was begging God to take his life before Jezebel did it for him. For forty days he cowered in the haunts of a windswept nowhere land – this mighty man of God who with his own eyes had seen bread multiply in a widow's kitchen and a dead man shake with new life in his grip.

Troubled, scared, and tired of fighting, Elijah wrestled with a prophet's worst torment: not knowing where to turn, not hearing God's voice, not being sure if he could trust his spiritual senses.

That's when God met him in his melancholy.

Yet even though the Lord spoke in a "still small voice," he didn't exactly join Elijah in feeling sorry for himself. His words wouldn't have comforted just anyone. In fact, they're very similar to the tone of Jesus' words to John the Baptist's disciples when John was questioning whether

Jesus was really who He said He was (see Matt 11:1-6). Instead of addressing Elijah's pressing concerns, God told him about a couple of kings He wanted him to anoint, as well as a prophet named Elisha who'd be taking over for him when he was gone.

Yes, God knows when to comfort, but He also knows when to confront. He knows when it's time to quit pouting, to get up and get busy. Because God's plan is what's important. His eternal Kingdom is what matters. And God knows that's what truly motivates a genuine worshiper like Elijah.

It's what gave this prickly prophet the guts to stand in King Ahab's face and tell him he was dead wrong about coveting Naboth's vineyard and covering it up with murder (1 Kgs 21). It's what helped him stand unruffled by King Ahaziah's blithering attempts at defying God's authority (2 Kgs 1). It's why he gladly asked the Lord that "a double portion of his spirit" rest upon his successor, Elisha – because being outperformed doesn't hinder someone whose only concern is that God's will is accomplished.

And it's what he got to see for himself when a fiery chariot swung low to the earth, and rode him through a dazzling whirlwind to glory.

Reasonable Worship

Dan Scott

We only learn to
behave ourselves in the
presence of God.

~ C.S. Lewis

St. Paul famously says that we should not be conformed to this world, but that we should be transformed by the renewing of our minds. He says that this is our "rational worship."

I know; the King James Version renders the phrase "reasonable service." But the phrase does not mean something like "this is the least one can do." Here, both the word "reasonable" and the word "service" have different meanings than how we normally use them. Here, "reasonable" is to be understood as "involving the use of reason." The word "service" on the other hand, is meant to be understood in the same way as, "I went to the service at Central Church last week." This makes Paul's use of the phrase "reasonable service" mean "worship that involves reason."

So if we are transformed by the "renewing of our mind," then somehow our rational being must participate in worship. Worship has to piece our reason with something that will force it to reflect, conclude, and act. Most of the time, simple reminders of our mortality, our need for grace, and the greatness of God are what do this for us. These are basic things that we tend to forget and that we should rehearse in worship.

Legend has it that the ancient city of Ephesus was built around a spring. People came from all around to drink from it and to bathe in its waters. Slowly a town grew up around the spring. As the centuries went by, however, the city fathers decided to charge tourists who came to drink or bathe there. So they built buildings over the spring. Other businesses and trades grew up around it, made a town, and finally the site of the original spring was forgotten.

Individuals are like that. As childhood comes to an end, we just know that things will be different for us. We will not waste life. We will accomplish great things. We will be happy. After a few years as adults, we know that painful reality will burst most of the fantasies that we envisioned in the springtime of our lives.

Our journey from idealism to cold rationality and then to perfunctory performance is a story as old as the human race. God created us for greatness and the original spring of divine vision for our lives bubbles deep within our souls. As time goes on, though, "life" tends to cover up the wellsprings of Life.

- Reasonable Worship -
Dan Scott

120

That is the human backdrop against which the gospel is proclaimed. Jesus came into the world to put us back on track to becoming all He created us to be. He died for us and made it possible for us to return to our eternal purpose. So becoming a Christian means becoming a new creature. We are not suddenly translated up to heaven but we are being transformed by the renewing of our minds.

Both Jesus and Paul spoke often about the gift of repentance. The word simply means a "change of mind." Repentance is a moment of choice when we face the crossroads and decide to go in a different direction than the one we had been traveling. This happens when our reason gets confronted by a truth that dispels the errors of our lives.

St. Paul is claiming that only a change of mind can lead to a transformation of character. There is no other way. In our day of lazy intellects, even Christians will claim that lasting change comes only from emotional experience, but that just isn't true. We appreciate emotional experience but lasting change comes from choices we make in our minds. Emotional experience may upset our normal routine enough to make us hunger for new life but real change always involves a choice.

We don't really worship until we get quiet enough for our minds to hear the engrafted word of God which is able to save our souls.

Only the Dance

Laurie Klein

The deepest level of worship is praising God in spite of pain, thanking God during a trial, trusting him when tempted, surrendering while suffering, and loving him when he seems distant.

~ Rick Warren

Several years ago I took a sacred dance class that changed my life. Brothers and sisters, I "got down." Talk about freedom!

Immediately afterward I broke my toe.

As the weeks passed, rather than ebbing, the initial pain squared itself. My left shoe was a vise; the bed sheet alone weighed twenty pounds. I forgot those dance steps. Two of my toes turned bluish-black. Although icy to the touch, they felt like they'd been doused with kerosene, set ablaze, then plugged into a 220-volt outlet. I couldn't use the foot, and foreboding (fear's second cousin once-removed) whispered of tumors, MS, paralysis.

"No," I staunchly said. God was allowing this pain for my growth. I pictured myself thin and beatifically pale, God's poster-girl for longsuffering, oozing character as my inspired visitors waited with me for Oprah's call.

It took several doctors several months to diagnose RSD. By then, I'd lost the sense of where my foot was in space and sprained my ankle. I disassociated, began calling it The Foot, as if it had mutinied. It spastically jerked away from contact with anything: a sock, a towel, a touch. My limp, akin to Chester's on *Gunsmoke*, progressed to the death-lurch of Quasimodo.

If you followed dancer/singer Paula Abdul's struggle with the same condition, you know that, neurologically, RSD impairs the body's ability to transmit and receive messages within muscles and tendons. The body believes it's wounded even after the triggering injury, usually a broken bone, has healed. Not unlike bitterness or unbelief, it can spread, affecting other parts of the body which, in extreme cases, atrophy. With RSD, miscommunication is involuntary. For the believer who steels his or her heart against hope (a common response to pain, grief, or disappointment), the result is similar: the still small voice that directs our days is gagged and, eventually, silenced.

Meanwhile, I was ordered to use my foot (it ground like eggshells under my weight) because otherwise, I'd lose it. Recovery evolved slowly, thanks to grace, grit, and some really good drugs. Over those two years I learned to offset pain by being stubbornly grateful. Forget Pollyana piety. Gut-level gratitude counts blessings without denying realities; it does the math but imagines solutions. It dismantles my "Yes, Lord, but…" fretting and fosters instead my "Yes, Lord, and…" response. It stays willing and soft and open to God, in spite of circumstances. Because it springs from love, thankfulness overrules fear. And this leads to wonder, which, once it has filled me up, overflows into worship. It helps me make my way to the Maker who reassures me I'm loved, whether I'm strong or weak. I have sometimes believed this whole hours at a time.

Like worship, gratitude is a present-tense practice. God is the great I AM, not I Was or I Might Be. When engaged in saying thank you to a sovereign God unaltered by time, I disengage from regret as well as foreboding. Gratitude makes the most of the moment; makes peace with the past; makes prayerful plans for tomorrow.

This is not to say I live there. Angst surfaces; hissy-fits happen. To counteract my alter-Eeyore I keep a gratitude book where I scribble my appreciation for small things each day. Well, most days.

After seven pain-free years my RSD recently reappeared in the same foot. You'd think I'd know by now to amp up the gratitude, but I thrashed through old feelings of anger and fear. There is an 8th century dance that Christians once did through cathedral labyrinths: the Tripudium. Three steps forward, one step back, it symbolizes human progress and frailty. Once again, no matter how I feel – scared, inadequate, irritable – worship is both a choice and an action.

"Look de-e-e-p in my eyes," my father used to say. I'd balance two bare feet on his shiny, brown wingtips. The room blurred as we spun. Our hearts were pounding. I couldn't move on my own, but his singular gaze steadied me. Violins did not sob in the background, nor did clouds of bubbles ascend. But the light, remembered now, seems golden.

As the poet, T. S. Eliot, said, *"Except for . . . the still point, there would be no dance, and there is only the dance."*

The Fourth Man
Audra Almond-Harvey

All of the wonder of
God happens right
above our arithmetic and
formula. The more I climb
outside my pat answers,
the more invigorating the
view, the more my heart
enters into worship.

~ Donald Miller

It is not always easy to worship with our lives and minds and hearts. There are so many distractions that pull our attention away from our Maker. Our minds quickly and logically justify the lapse of focus – there are demands placed on us from all sides, there is pain in life to be faced, and often it takes all we have to just barely stay afloat.

I remember hearing the story of Shadrach, Meshach, and Abednego as a child. I admired them for their faith even then. They turned down real riches and real prestige out of allegiance to God. They didn't just face losing all they had earned but they faced losing their very lives. The danger was not just real, it was actual – by the middle of the chapter they are *actually* in the furnace.

I went through a very difficult time a few years ago which forced me to question myself and my faith. Through this story, God taught me how to endure and how to honor Him by doing so. When I was taught as a child about the fiery furnace, we always skipped to the end of the chapter. "God will reward you for your obedience," my pastor said, referencing their reward from the king after they were pulled from the furnace. And while they were rewarded, they were *in* the fire first. You cannot look at their experience and think, "Now *there* was a good opportunity for promotion." Who would literally throw away everything and allow themselves to be flung into a bonfire for a raise? No one would, as we know that there is no likelihood of survival.

Shadrach, Meshach, and Abednego knew something that made them able to withstand their fate. They knew that though they might be facing their death, God could deliver them. They made a proclamation that still stops me short:

> "If we are thrown into the blazing furnace, the God we serve is able to save us from it, and He **will** rescue us from your hand, O king. **But even if He does not**, we want you to know, O king, that we will not serve your gods or worship the image of gold you have set up." (Dan 3:17-18, NIV, emphasis added)

This statement is profound. Such a bold illustration of faith! First, it says that God is able to bring deliverance. This is a key to worship. To worship God we must first believe that what God says about Himself is true. Second, their statement says that He will rescue them. But then they seem to contradict themselves: they say that even if He does not rescue them, they will not bow.

They did not refuse to bow because they knew they would survive the fire. They refused because of their allegiance to God. Their faith in the truth of His nature was more permanent to them than their lives. They knew that even if they died, they would be with God. And that no matter how much they endured to be with Him, it would be worth it.

Choosing to worship God through pain and struggle is a difficult choice. It is these times that make us put our trust not in what we see or feel, but in His words and in who He says He is. But we must also be sure not to worship anything else. They could have bowed. Who would have known? Who would have judged them? After all, everyone else was bowing. No one else wanted to be thrown in the furnace. Besides: it was just a meaningless physical motion; God knew they didn't really *mean* it. Surely God would have understood and forgiven – their *lives* were on the line!

But here is the real key. Worshiping in truth requires being aware that our choices define us, and that God isn't blind. He knows our struggle and that what He asks of us is challenging, but He asks it all the same and our call is to obey. The seemingly insignificant choices that separate us little by little from God will inevitably lead to a lack of intimacy with Him.

We can't give up, even if no one else will know that we did. We cannot hide in a life of apparent virtue. But we *can* take the struggle and the pain to God, and let Him take it as proof of our praise. Anyone can say "God is good, all the time" when life is easy. It is far harder when the words cost you, when you must choose to say them and believe them to be true when everything you see says He has left you.

We must not overlook the truth that God revealed in the fire. There was a fourth man who walked with them. When difficulties surround you, rejoice, because you serve a God who will not let you walk them alone.

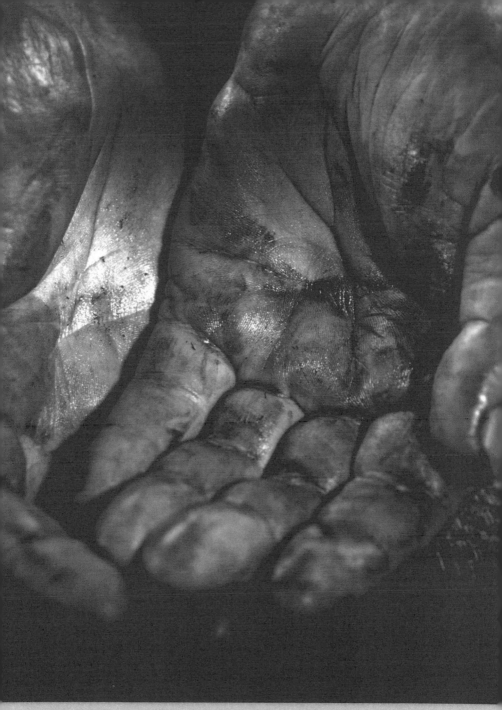

Nehemiah

Lawrence Kimbrough

To understand the depth of Nehemiah's devotion to God, His people, and His covenant, you have to try putting yourself in his place.

Imagine you're a respected leader in your local community, rubbing shoulders with the most influential people in town, able to walk into the statehouse and be called by your first name. But one day, an old family friend asks if he can get an appointment to come see you. Something about a problem in the town where your great-great-grandfather was born (wherever that is): economic slowdown, unemployment, general malaise.

It would probably have been noble enough just to promise you'd look into it, maybe send someone down to observe the situation or agree to talk to your friends in government about some kind of federal aid. "Come by again next time you're in town."

Imagine instead that on hearing the news, your lip begins to quiver, tears well in your eyes. For days, you don't eat, trying to hear from God what you should do.

That's the heart of Nehemiah.

He had a trusted position in daily contact with the king of the Persian Empire, living 140 years and four or five generations away from his family's homeland. But somebody – perhaps his mom or dad or grandfather – somebody had made sure he knew who he was, that he knew where his worship belonged. They had taught him about lamb's blood on the doorposts and a flight into the Egyptian night, about a wall of water that turned the Red Sea into a red carpet and a fiery finger that carved tablets of stone on Sinai.

Nehemiah's feet walked the halls of Persian palaces. But his eyes were drawn to a southern window and a land in the distance he'd never seen. Jerusalem, the City of God, the one true God. *His* God.

And he was going. To save it. With God's help, the God who had promised *"no matter how far away we were, we could turn to you and start obeying your laws. Then you would bring us back to the place where you have chosen to be worshiped." (Neh 1:9, CEV)*

So with the king's permission in hand and his building supplies on order, Nehemiah turned his back on royal refinements to rally a group of disheartened, repatriated exiles to rebuild the city walls.

Now that's a big job all by itself. It's even harder when you're spending half your time fighting off the annoying armies of paranoid politicians. But Nehemiah never flinched in the face of human opposition, because he knew God had bigger plans for this project than military defense and a sounder substructure.

Restoring the city of Jerusalem would restore the soul of Israel and re-knit the covenant link between God and His people.

That's what drove Nehemiah, even when the enthusiasm of his own countrymen melted into shrugs and sighs. That's why he re-established the laws of God in the land of Abraham, Isaac, and Jacob. That's why he ran out the money-grubbing foreigners who were teasing the people with their wares on the Sabbath. That's why he made sure the priests and temple workers were relieved of their financial burdens in order to perform the most important job in town: worshiping God.

The joy of the Lord would be their strength, or they would have no strength at all.

When Nehemiah had prayed back in Persia for a way to help Jerusalem, he never dreamed how personal God's answer would be. But the Lord knows that a man built for worship can build more than a wall. He can build up his family, his church, his leaders, his coworkers, his community.

Yes, Nehemiah, even his nation.

Never Give Up
J. Daniel Smith

How quickly we forget what
it's all about.
We can get so strategic
that we worship so our
church will grow, not because
He is worthy.
But we're doing all this
because God is worthy
and we want to worship Him.

~ Tommy Walker

Paul must have been keenly aware of the propensity of human nature to lose heart. Long-suffering, fortitude, and patience are, for most of us, not qualities that come easily. Nevertheless, in the work of the Kingdom it is imperative that we know how to function successfully when the wind is filling our sails as well as those times when we have to drag out the oars and row as hard as we can just to keep going. You can be certain that you'll experience both of these seasons – probably several times each – if you live long enough.

It was a Sunday afternoon as I was preparing to leave my home for the evening prayer service at church when I walked past the television in our bedroom and a story caught my eye. It was our local news station giving the account of a fine young high school student. As they were introducing him, they showed only his face as he talked about his love for running in the track program at school.

It was easy to see that he was very bright, articulate, and quite a handsome young fellow with a very intelligent look in his eye. Then as the camera panned out, it became evident what made this story so unique. He had been seriously handicapped by some crippling disease that came upon him as a child. His legs were very frail and barely able to hold him up even when just standing. His arms also were withered and drawn. Yet deep within his heart was an insatiable desire to be a runner, regardless of the physical handicaps he faced.

The story went on to show him running in several races. It was painful to watch as he fell to the ground time and time again, often bleeding from his chest and face, as he could not brace himself from the fall due to his withered arms. He entered every race knowing full well he would come in last – dead last. He entered every race completely realizing he would fall several times and most of the falls would cause him to encounter pain. How graphic it was to see the pained look on his face as someone would help him back to his feet to continue the race. Just then, the camera went to a shot of his coach who said of the young man, "The amazing thing about him is that he has never failed to finish a race! All the pain he faces in a race is worth it to him just to cross the finish line."

I will admit to you that I stood there and cried like a baby, partly out of guilt for the times I've given up when the going got rough and partly out of a sense of identifying with the young man. I, too, know what it is to be in a race for which I'm not really qualified, yet wanting so badly just to be in the race. I also know what it is to come in last – dead last.

As I drove on to church that evening, tears streaming down my face, I renewed my commitment to finish the race regardless of what pain I may encounter along the way. Somehow I think it's a decision that every believer has to make – deciding that crossing the finish line, hearing the "well done" from our Savior is worth every ounce of pain we may have to endure.

It will be worth it all when we see Jesus.
Life's trials will seem so small when we see Christ.
One glimpse of His dear face, all sorrow will erase;
so bravely run the race 'til we see Christ.

Words and music to "When We See Christ" by Esther Kerr Rusthoi.

Overwhelmed?

Patrick Tharp

Without worship, we go
about miserable.

~ A.W. Tozer

King David is described in Acts 13:22 as *"a man after God's own heart."* That is an awesome testimony to a man who went from his father's sheepfold to the throne of a nation and led them in their golden age. He was not a perfect man, but he had a perfect heart of love for his God. The more I read the Psalms, the greater appreciation I have for him and his fellowship and intimacy with the Lord. David faced many enemies in his day. Enemies without, enemies within. But he always found his refuge in the arms of the Lord and in the comfort of His presence. He even learned how to find his strength in God in the middle of terrible situations.

Jesus encouraged his disciples by saying, *"These things I have spoken to you, that in Me you may have peace. In the world you have tribulation: but take courage; I have overcome the world." (Jn 16:33, NASB)* We will have tribulation. It's not a question of *if* but of *when* and *how long*. We all will go through it. Trials, testing, and tribulation can sometimes cause our hearts to get weighed down, can cause us to lose our eternal perspective, and can ultimately overwhelm us. Being overwhelmed can cause us to literally faint or give up in the face of adversity. But trials can actually work for our benefit in God's eternal scheme of things.

David was facing this in Psalm 143. He started by crying out to the Lord. The enemy was persecuting his soul, to the point where David felt like his life had been cast down to the ground and he was dwelling in darkness among the dead. Ever been there or felt like that? David was so overwhelmed that he said his heart within was desolate. The man who enjoyed such sweet communion with the Father was now in a season of appalling desolation and great horror. But even here, the light and hope of the Lord broke through.

The Holy Spirit showed David and shows us what to do when our hearts are overwhelmed. Psalm 143:5 says, *"I remember the days of old."* David was not remembering the good old days as somehow magically better than the present, as many are tempted to, but rather he was remembering the days of God's faithfulness to him. He was reminding himself of how the Lord came through before.

1 Chronicles 16:12 encourages us to, *"remember his marvelous works that he has done, his wonders, and the judgments of his mouth."* Charles Spurgeon said that these thoughts are *"as flowers for the bees of faith to visit, from which they may make honey for present use."* On a regular basis, we need to intentionally remind ourselves of the Lord's consistent faithfulness, mercy, love, and truth in our lives. That's why so much of the Bible deals with remembering.

In Psalm 143:6 David says, *"I stretch forth my hands unto thee."* We see two things in this verse. First, that David the warrior was also a worshiper. Worshiping the Lord frees us from our circumstance and connects us with our Creator, who is so much bigger. Worship needs to be offered especially when we don't feel like it or our hearts are heavy. Nothing chases away the gloom of being overwhelmed like communion with God.

Secondly, as we stretch out our hands it is an act of faith. Even though outward circumstances may appear not to have changed, we know that we are to walk by faith, not by sight. And as we reach out in faith, the Lord is always faithful to meet us there as our very present help in times of trouble. That is the place where withered hands and hearts are made whole by the power of Jesus. Our God is in the business of restoring withered, worn, troubled, and overwhelmed hearts and homes.

So if you find yourself feeling lost and overwhelmed, remember the days of God's faithfulness. Meditate on His works, stretch out your hand in faith and worship and experience the quickening power of Jesus. And remember: God is faithful.

When the Pressure's on... WORSHIP

Ken Abraham

The Church is the Church in her worship.

Worship is not an optional extra, but is of the very life and essence of the Church...

Man is never more truly man than when he worships God. He rises to all the heights of human dignity when he worships God, and all God's purpose in Creation and in Redemption are fulfilled in us as together in worship we are renewed in and through Christ, and in the name of Christ we glorify God.

~ James B. Torrance

Worship and worry are incompatible concepts. You can worship God in the face of your problems, trusting that He will work out His will, or you can worry about how you are going to handle your circumstances, but you can't do both.

A fascinating illustration of this is recorded three times in the Old Testament (2 Kgs 18-19; 2 Chron 32:1-23; and Is 36-37). God's people, led by King Hezekiah, were being held under siege by King Sennacherib of Assyria. The enemy had seized the major fortified cities of Judah, and the Assyrians were now pressuring Jerusalem, the capital city. Sennacherib demanded a hefty ransom from God's people and then sent his emissary, Rabshakeh, to intimidate Hezekiah into making a deal. Each day Rabshakeh stood outside the city walls, insulting Hezekiah, God, and His people.

When Hezekiah's representatives met with Rabshakeh, he railed against them, *"What is this confidence you have? You say that you have counsel and strength for war, but those are empty words."* Rabshakeh bluffed, *"And have I now come up without the Lord's approval against this land to destroy it? The Lord said to me, 'Go up against this land and destroy it.'"* *(2 Kgs 18:25, NASB)*

The audacity of this guy, telling God's people that the Lord sent him there to destroy them. Talk about bold! Hezekiah's representatives attempted to prevent God's people from hearing Rabshakeh's insults by requesting that he speak Aramaic rather than Hebrew, but Rabshakeh refused. He raised his voice and ranted all the more, presenting three "reasons" why God's people should submit.

First, he roared, *"Hear the word of the great king, the king of Assyria...'Do not let Hezekiah deceive you, for he will not be able to deliver you from my hand; nor let Hezekiah make you trust in the Lord, saying, 'The Lord will surely deliver us, and this city shall not be given into the hand of the king of Assyria.'"* *(2 Kgs 18:28-30, NASB)*

Second, Rabshakeh tempted, "Come make a bargain, make your peace with me. We'll take good care of you. We'll give you food to eat, a land of bread and vineyards. Each of you can have your own place where you can live it up!" No doubt, the enemy's deal appealed to the tired, hungry people listening on the wall.

Finally, Rabshekeh rationalized, "Look, have any of the gods of other nations delivered anyone from the hand of the king of Assyria? No way!" Understand, Satan's representatives will tell you anything, if it will keep you from trusting God and will cause you to cave under pressure.

Hezekiah had warned God's people not to do verbal battle with the enemy, and the people obeyed Hezekiah's command. When the king heard Rabshakeh's evil messages, he tore his clothes and covered himself with sackcloth, signs of grief and humility before God. Then Hezekiah prayed.

No doubt, had Hezekiah started wringing his hands in worry and despair, the battle would have been lost. But Hezekiah didn't do that. Instead, he submitted to God and testified of God's greatness. Notice, too, he resisted the enemy by refusing to respond in foolish verbal confrontations; then he diffused the enemy's threats by taking them to the Lord in prayer. Hezekiah didn't begin by outlining his woeful dilemma to God, but by worshiping God. He said, *"O Lord, the God of Israel, who art enthroned above the cherubim, Thou art the God, Thou alone, of all the kingdoms of the earth. Thou hast made heaven and earth."* (2 Kgs 19:15, NASB)

With the devil beating on his door, Hezekiah paused to worship the Lord, and to testify of His awesome power before asking Him for help. Then he sent for Isaiah, hoping that the prophet would have a word from the Lord.

Isaiah did. He told the king, *"Thus says the Lord, 'Do not be afraid because of the words that you have heard, with which the servants of the king of Assyria have blasphemed Me. Behold, I will put a spirit in him so that he shall hear a rumor and return to his own land. And I will make him fall by the sword in his own land.'"* (Is 37:6-7, NASB)

Shortly after this, Sennacherib mysteriously received word that Babylon was rebelling. He abandoned his siege of Jerusalem and headed his army homeward. But God wasn't finished with Sennacherib. Nobody blasphemes God and gets away with it. *"Then the angel of the Lord went out and struck 185,000 in the camp of the Assyrians; and when men arose early in the morning, behold, all of these were dead."* (Is 37:36, NASB) Notice that one angel destroyed 185,000 of the enemy's finest warriors overnight! Remember: *"The angel of the Lord encamps around those who fear Him." (Ps 34:7)* That fear is not the cowering fear of a child against a bully. No, quite the contrary, this sort of fear is the awesome honor and respect and adoration offered to God in true worship.

Sennacherib returned home defeated and was murdered by his own sons. Hezekiah and the people of God won a great victory by surrendering the battle to the Lord, placing their focus on worshiping the God who could answer in power and might.

When the pressure comes, don't wring your hands in despair and frustration. Go to God in humble worship and praise, acknowledging your confidence in Him. He will work supernatural miracles if necessary to deliver you from the hands of your enemies. Your top priority is to keep your focus on God, not your problems; to worship Him rather than worry or fret. As you do, relax and expect to experience His presence in a most unusual way.

Simeon

Lawrence Kimbrough

Everything we know about Simeon springs from 11 short verses in Luke, chapter 2. That's it. And then he's never heard from again. But if you only had 11 verses to leave behind – 11 verses to sum up your life, your character, and your depth of worship – you'd take Simeon's in a heartbeat.

Perhaps he was a man of few words anyway. A man of deep, ponderous thoughts, of devout, unwavering worship but not of long, drawn-out conversation. Nothing suggests that his life was even remotely spectacular. We might have read his story with the same passion that drives us to Leviticus for our morning devotions. Might have come in handy at bedtime...

But the Bible says he was a good man. And he loved God.

And he was waiting . . . waiting . . . waiting . . . waiting to see something he had read about in the Prophets for as long as he could remember, something God had promised him personally that he would see before he died:

> "'Behold, the days are coming,' says the LORD, 'that I will raise to David a Branch of righteousness; a King shall reign and prosper, and execute judgment and righteousness in the earth. In His days Judah will be saved, And Israel will dwell safely; Now this is His name by which He will be called: The Lord Our Righteousness.'" (Jer 23:5-6, NKJV)

Waiting. Waiting on Jesus. That was the theme of Simeon's worship.

But waiting can be boring, discouraging, maddening. It can tease your hopes, toy with your assumptions, jam the signals on your spiritual progress. It's not the best way to get people at church to notice you.

Yet even when his heart told him he was kidding himself, Simeon clung to God through the restlessness. And for every time he tightened his grip on the invisible hand of faith, that's how much sweeter the fulfillment was when it finally arrived.

Simeon learned that faithfulness is the purest form of worship.

Imagine what went through his mind that incredible day. He couldn't have known with 100 percent certainty that it was a baby he was looking for. There was no nametag embroidered on Jesus' blanket. Who knows how many times he'd tottered into town before and spotted someone who arrested his attention . . . and he wondered. All the more reason why that special morning could have raised the same familiar doubts in his mind.

But a man full of the Spirit, who's lived long enough to love the Lord with all his heart and soul and mind and strength, he recognizes God's voice when He speaks. And while everyone around him was lost in the hum and small talk of their daily activity, oblivious to the fact that the object of their worship was in the temple, in the flesh, Simeon saw his Messiah.

So glorious and enraptured was his worship of the Christ child, it even caught Mary and Joseph by surprise. Like Simeon, they knew who their baby was. They also knew he was keeping them up nights, going through diapers as fast as they could wash them. Real life was setting in. But Simeon's worship was so full, so authentic, its awe rubbed off on a young carpenter and his new bride. There they stood, the three of them, lost in the unity that comes from genuine worship.

Now Simeon could die in peace. He could look back on a life of waiting, following, and faithfulness, and say that nothing had been wasted. Because of God's grace, every moment had served a purpose.

His waiting was over. His worship had just begun.

Trust and Obey

Kimberlee Stone

The instinct to worship is
hardly less strong than
the instinct to eat.

~ Dorothy Thompson

Have you ever taken a plane ride on an overcast day? The kind of day where clouds encircle your every move and you know there will be turbulence, yet there's nothing you can do about it? Recently I boarded a plane on just that kind of day, much to my apprehension. For a person who breaks out in sweaty palms the moment her foot hits the carpeted floor of any Boeing 757, clouds are not a joke. My nerves get a bit loopy the moment I enter an airport before I fly. I just don't do well sitting on an undersized seat surrounded by strangers in a contraption whose aerodynamics I cannot quite grasp. The act of even boarding a plane is a small testament of how much I trust God.

On this day, the "Fasten Seatbelts" sign was illuminated immediately into our flight. It remained illuminated for longer than normal. Almost instantly, a flight attendant called out overhead, "Please remain seated until we are able to get beyond the bad weather." Now who would want to get up, only to be knocked to their feet in front of people they'd never see again? Thank you, I thought to myself, but I will stay buckled up for the entire flight!

As we ascended, thick and threatening gray clouds engulfed the plane. The bumps started out small, then varied as we traveled; a jiggle here and there, followed by a life-size dip that caused the plane's engines to moan loudly. At least in my mind. It would be about this time in every flight when the seconds turn into minutes. I hold my breath, close my eyes, recite every scripture that comes to mind, and sing every simple worship chorus I can think of to soothe my overly panicky heart. Why does it take so long to find smooth air? Eventually it feels as though the powdery clouds are coming full force at the window from which I casually glance in prayerful anticipation that it will be over soon.

Then, unexpectedly and instantaneously, calm overtakes the plane. The wings find their composure, the seatbelt sign goes off with a "ding," and with a skeptical reach of my shaky (and still sweaty) hand, I muster the courage to look out the window. Expecting to see more dismal shades of dreariness in the sky, I am shaken, caught off guard, when my eyes behold the peaceful sky.

It is difficult to explain, but that color is more than just the blue found in a child's box of crayons. It is vibrant and rich. It stretches as far as my eyes can see. It is unadulterated and soft. Against the clouds below, it looks fluorescent, like it would glow right through the darkest part of the darkest night. As tranquility joins the flight, passengers begin mulling about the cabin. My palms are cool. Finally.

I am gently reminded that my newfound revelation mirrors how we walk in trust and obedience with God. We start the journey by saying, "God, you are in control. I'm scared, but I trust you." Then a few clouds come our way and we kick into fright mode as if God has left us abandoned like a puppy in the rain. The storm comes with clouds, like the ones that encroached upon the plane, and the ride turns treacherous. Big bumps; huge problems. We hear the whisper of God say, "Trust me," while we battle fear that quickly overtakes our minds.

We say to Him, "Yes, but my husband just left me. How am I going to make it?" Or, "I've been hurt so badly, I cannot find an ounce of joy left in me. I love you God, but I can't trust you with this. I have to do it on my own."

Again, God echoes, "Trust me." We even become so bold as to sing something like, *"Tis so sweet to trust in Jesus. Just to take Him at His word…"* But face it. Life gets so scary sometimes that we forget the words.

Rest assured. Like the ever present "Fasten Your Seatbelts" sign which is certain to light up during every flight, God fills our hearts with worship that comforts us in our greatest time of need. Sometimes it is with a weak voice, sitting in seat 5H, that we continue with, *"I'm so glad I learned to trust Thee, precious Jesus, Savior, friend; and I know that Thou are with me, wilt be with me to the end."*

He strengthens us for the journey. And restores us. It is only His infinite mercy and love that helps us rise above our adversity like a jet making its way through the turbulence. As we learn to trust Him and worship Him in all things, the ride becomes enjoyable and the sky turns a shade of blue that is more stunning than any we've ever experienced before.

"Tis So Sweet to Trust in Jesus" words by Louisa M. R. Stead; music by William J. Kirkpatrick.

Simple
Caleb Quaye

The object of man's worship, whatever it be, will naturally be his standard of perfection. He clothes it with every attribute belonging, in his view, to a perfect character; and this character he himself endeavors to attain.

~ Simon Greenleaf

Jesus said that in order to enter the Kingdom of Heaven one should have a childlike faith (not childish). This speaks so much of simplicity and purity in terms of motives, thought and actions.

With this in mind, the metaphor I think best describes the kind of worship that touches the heart of the Father is when young children are learning to draw. All of their attention is focused on creating a picture that they can't wait to present to Mom and Dad. Some kids paint or scribble frantically because they are nearly overcome with excitement at the prospect of giving something they have created. Others take a long time to complete the project because they want to make it as perfect as they can in order to please their parents. The simple yet profound motive behind both methods is that the children love their parents and will do anything they can with their newly discovered creative gifts to express that love.

The joy of offering our love to the Father in the form of artistic creativity or simply living life with Him in mind is deep within us. It is a joy that longs for completion. The completion of this joy is simply to hear the Father saying to the child "that's great," "that's wonderful," "can you make me another one?" and "thank you so much."

Someone once said that our worship is like the pictures that God loves to stick on His refrigerator. I like that. When we get to heaven we hope to hear from Jesus the words "Well done good and faithful servant," meaning we had been faithful to live a life that reflected His character, where worship was at the center.

The Greek word for worship (proskuneo) means to kiss like a dog licking his master's hand. This kiss is a response to passion; it is not something that is analytically thought through. We kiss because we love, plain and simple. It is the same passion with which the child creates the painting.

In our complicated churches there are never ending debates over issues of worship and style, trends in worship, cultural relevance in worship, traditional versus contemporary worship, alternative and emerging church worship, loud or soft worship, Boomer, Gen-X, or Millennial worship... On and on it goes in the endless circles of fear and formula, trying to arrive at the perfect definition that will satisfy all theological positions and institutional insecurities. But it's not supposed to be that complicated.

"Then He turned to the woman and said to Simon, 'Do you see this woman? I entered your house; you gave Me no water for My feet, but she has washed My feet with her tears and wiped them with the hair of her head. You gave Me no kiss, but this woman has not ceased to kiss My feet since the time I came in. You did not anoint My head with oil, but this woman has anointed My feet with fragrant oil. Therefore I say to you, her sins, which are many, are forgiven, for she loved much. But to whom little is forgiven, the same loves little.' Then He said to her, 'Your sins are forgiven.'" (Lk 7:44-48, NKJV)

Worship "in spirit and in truth" has nothing to do with style or formula. It does, however, have everything to do with being the most creative kiss that we can offer, because all of our faculties are focused on the Lamb of God who came to take away the sins of the world and deliver us from darkness. Having brought us on over into His Kingdom, we are eternally free to simply say "thank you" with a kiss.

Call Upon the Name of the Lord
Jeff Ferguson

Worship is first and
foremost for His benefit,
not ours, though it is
marvelous to discover
that in giving Him
pleasure, we ourselves
enter into what can
become our richest
and most wholesome
experience in life.

~ Graham Kendrick

My mother was three months pregnant with me when my biological father drowned. He was eighteen years old. My despondent mother left her home in Flint, Michigan and traveled to the rural mountains of North Carolina where my father was from. She met his mother, Granny, for the first time two days before the funeral. That's when my Granny first found out she had a grandbaby on the way. The two hurting women found comfort in each other's company, so my mother stayed in the mountains with Granny until I was born.

Later on, my mother and I moved home to Flint, Michigan where she became a waitress at the Ambassador Coney Island on the city's south side. We were dirt poor, so often in lieu of babysitting my mother would bring me to work with her. When I was six years old and perched upon the soda counter, an older man came and sat next to me. I liked him immediately because he had a southern accent like Granny and the people I loved from the mountains.

"What's your name, son?" he asked with hillbilly in his voice.

"My name is little Jeffie Crump." I replied.

"What are you doin' out here tonight, young man?"

"It's Saturday night, so my mamma and me... we're out huntin' daddies! Do you wanna be my daddy?!" I smiled.

Red-faced and looking around to see who could hear us, he blurted out, "Where's your mamma?" I pointed her out and a happy look came upon his face...they got married a few months later.

What my mamma and I didn't know on that Saturday night we met my new dad was that he was an old-fashioned, Pentecostal pastor. He adopted me the next year when I was seven years old and my name became Jeff Ferguson. It took me half of second grade to learn how to spell Ferguson. Our house, the church parsonage, was actually connected to the church sanctuary. I very literally grew up in church.

And our church was *strict*!

There were many things I was not allowed to do that other kids my age could do. Dad was extremely firm on a couple of issues in particular. One of those issues I'm very thankful for. Dad would never let us say the name "Jesus" casually or in vain. He taught us that if we said the name of Jesus too casually, His name would lose its "specialness" in our lives. (Dad was country and often would make up words that he thought were real.) If we said His name in a loose way without purpose, we were in danger of losing the belief in the power His name could bring.

My dad taught us that in the name of Jesus, you could speak to sickness or disease in a loved one's body and that sickness or disease would unravel itself from around the tissue of that body and would have to leave. Dad said you could speak to the storm in someone's life and command that storm to cease in the "name of Jesus" so the person who had been in anguish could lay their head on their pillow that night in perfect peace. My dad taught us that every demon, every attack, every name, had to bow to the name of Jesus. He told us all the authority of heaven backs up the believer who uses the name of Jesus.

My dad would also preach, "Whosoever calls upon the name of the Lord shall be saved." It doesn't matter if they keep the rules of this church or even if this church agrees with them or their doctrine. If they simply call upon the name of the Lord they shall be saved! If they call upon the name of the Lord they shall be delivered!

To this day I only say the name of Jesus on purpose for a purpose. I understand the power of His holy name. I respect and honor the name of Jesus. My dad has been in heaven for nine years. I thank God he taught me how to call upon the name of the Lord.

"And it shall come to pass, that whosoever shall call on the name of the Lord shall be delivered..." (Jl 2:32, KJV)

"And whatsoever ye shall ask in my name, that will I do, that the Father may be glorified in the Son. If ye shall ask any thing in my name, I will do it." (Jn 14: 13-14, KJV)

"And being found in fashion as a man, he humbled himself, and became obedient unto death, even the death of the cross. Wherefore God also hath highly exalted him, and given him a name which is above every name: That at the name of Jesus every knee should bow, of things in heaven, and things in earth, and things under the earth; And that every tongue should confess that Jesus Christ is Lord, to the glory of God the Father." (Phil 2:8-11, KJV)

John the Baptist

Lawrence Kimbrough

John the Baptist may have received the most daunting assignment in the entire Bible: to subdue man's most stubborn enemy – a foe more tenacious than David's Goliath, more swarming than Samson's Philistines.

For John to succeed in his mission, he would have to pick up the axe in his own hands and chop down the wild, natural growth of his own pride, pulverize every blade and branch of ambition, stop his own ego, and slay his own self.

Worship would not be an easy choice for him, an inexpensive side-item. It would cost him an arm and a leg...and a head on Herod's platter.

Less understanding philosophers might look at the story of John the Baptist and say life was cruel to him, that he was forced to cross a fatal line in history which short-circuited his effectiveness and ruined his search for personal meaning and purpose.

But John's purpose was to point people to Jesus.

> "There comes One after me who is mightier than I, whose sandal strap I am not worthy to stoop down and loose." (Mk 1:7, NKJV)

> "This was He of whom I said, 'He who comes after me is preferred before me, for He was before me." (Jn 1:15, NKJV)

> "He must increase, but I must decrease." (Jn 3:30, NKJV)

And decrease he did.

Jesus' arrival at the Jordan River effectively ended the ministry of John the Baptist. Though he would continue railing against the hypocrisies of the religious establishment and baptizing those who were truly sorry for their sins, the crowds would dwindle. The long lines would disappear. The interest in a long-haired, locust-eating, fire-breathing street preacher from the backwoods would melt in the shadow of an even more novel attraction: a carpenter's son from Nazareth who claimed to be the Son of God.

And John would have to watch from the sidelines, his purpose completed, his mission accomplished at just over 30 years of age.

That's when worship had to become tough: when the One you

worship is also the cousin who's just put you out of a job. To make things more difficult, you can imagine John's own disciples probably weren't so content with their newfound lack of influence. Surely they peppered him with questions about what to do next, how to stay in front of the people, why he was so certain this guy was the Lamb.

But John knew. And in humility, he graciously stepped aside, having prepared the way for the Lord, having given *"knowledge of salvation to His people by the remission of their sins, through the tender mercy of our God." (Lk 1:77-78, NKJV)*

And the Lamb was pleased with His reception.

Perhaps they crossed paths again after the baptism. Perhaps he had a chance to feel Jesus' embrace and to hear with his own ears how grateful Jesus was for John's faithfulness to his calling. But while dying too young in a dank, drafty prison cell, John's life flashed before his eyes. Doubts and questions he had kept interred by faith began resurrecting with a frenzy. Desperate for answers, he tried to get a message through to Jesus: *"Are You the Coming One, or do we look for another?" (Matt 11:3, NKJV)*

See for yourself, John.

"The blind see and the lame walk; the lepers are cleansed and the deaf hear; the dead are raised up and the poor have the gospel preached to them." (Matt 11:5, NKJV)

His worship had been in the right place all along.

Why We Worship

Dr. David C. Cooper

When I admire the wonder of a sunset or the beauty of the moon, my soul expands in worship of the Creator.

~ Mahatma Gandhi

Why should we love God exclusively? Is God on some kind of a cosmic ego-trip needing our constant attention so that He can feel good about Himself? Is God the Eternal Egotist?

This may shock you, but God doesn't *need* our love or worship. God *enjoys* our love and worship, but He doesn't need it. God is self-existent. He doesn't need anything. Worship is God's gift to us. *We're* the ones who need to worship. Worship guides us on the pathway to really knowing God.

We worship God for two reasons: Because of who He is and because of what He has done for us. Listen to the first commandment: *"I am the LORD your God, who brought you out of Egypt, out of the land of slavery. You shall have no other gods before me." (Ex 20:1-3, NIV)* It is because God brought us out of the slavery of sin that we are free to worship Him. True worship is our response of love to the love of God. We have been redeemed from the slavery of sin and set free.

God redeemed Israel from slavery in Egypt by His power, seen in parting the Red Sea, and by atonement of the Passover Lamb. God has also redeemed us from sin by the power of Christ's resurrection, by the blood of Jesus given for our sins on the cross.

Jesus fulfilled all the Old Testament expressions of redemption – the Passover, the Day of Atonement, and the Levitical offerings. *"Christ, our Passover lamb has been sacrificed." (1 Cor 5:7, NIV)* Redemption means, *"You are not your own you were bought at a price." (1 Cor 6:19-20, NIV)* We are no longer our own. Therefore, let us glorify God with our lives. Remember, your life is God's gift to you; what you do with your life is your gift to God.

We become what we worship. If we worship money, we become materialists. If we worship pleasure, we become hedonists. If we worship power, we control and manipulate others for our own ends. If we worship fame, we become gods in our own eyes. If we worship our abilities, we become humanists.

However, if we worship God in spirit and in truth, we become like Him. God made us in His image. Sin marred that image. Salvation renews the image of God in us. Worship causes us to mature in the image of our heavenly Father.

Worship brings the perfecting of character. *"And we...reflect the Lord's glory and are being transformed into his own image with ever-increasing splendor and this transformation comes from the Lord, who is the Spirit." (2 Cor 3:18, NIV)*

The word "reflect" can also be translated "behold." We reflect what we behold. David desired to worship God in the temple so that he might *"behold the beauty of the Lord." (Ps 27:4, NIV)*

While on a short-term mission trip, a North Carolina pastor by the name of Jack Hinton was leading a worship service at a leper colony on the island of Tobago. There was time for one more song, so he asked if anyone had a request. A woman who had her back facing the pulpit turned around. "It was the most hideous face I had ever seen," Hinton said. "Her nose and ears were completely gone. The disease had destroyed her lips as well. She lifted her fingerless hand in the air and asked, "Can we sing 'Count Your Many Blessings?'"

Overcome with emotion Hinton left the service. He was followed by a team member who said, "Jack, I guess you'll never be able to sing that song again."

"Yes, I will," Jack replied, "but I'll never sing it the same way."

Yet Will I Hope In Him
Angel Smythe

There is no "one-size-fits-all" approach to worship and friendship with God. One thing is certain: You don't bring glory to God by trying to be someone he never intended you to be. God wants you to be yourself.

~ Rick Warren

As I think about what it means to truly worship God, so many thoughts and visual images come to mind. I've been to many workshops and conferences and discussed so many facets of what it means to worship. I've been a worshiper ever since I can remember, and I've been a leader of worship for at least a dozen years.

As I've watched "worship" become a genre of music and a trendy, cool thing to do, I've frequently pondered the danger in relying on feelings. Music reaches to the depth of the heart and soul; it taps into emotions that can overtake us and cause us to transcend to new heights. As a worship leader and artist, I find that, because of my personality and God given design, I so often rely on how I feel when it comes to worshiping God. It is easy to think the worship time was great if it "felt" good. Growing up in Spirit-filled churches, there was no doubt when the Holy Spirit was at work because His presence could be felt all over the room. There was no denying His power.

But is God any less at work when we don't feel anything special going on?

I think I've finally just begun to understand the Job 13:15 concept of *"Though He slay me, yet will I trust in Him."* I've lived through some dark days. I found it easy initially to question God, and literally cry out to Him from a place in my heart of wondering if He was still at work while cognitively knowing that He is sovereign. Even Job spent time cursing the day he was born and felt like the purpose of his life and the joy he once knew had been cancelled out.

As I've recently faced some discouragement and sadness, I've found myself actually saying out loud, "Lord, I know and trust that You are at work in my life, though I can't see what is going on." Somehow, my lips were able to utter those words in the midst of my state of despair. For the first time, I wasn't relying on how I was feeling to trust that God was at work on my behalf. This is not a new concept to me, just a new initial response when things don't feel great.

I looked again at Job's life. From the beginning of the story, God presented him to Satan and asked if he'd considered Job as a target. God said that Job was a man of perfect integrity; no one else was like him. He feared God and turned away from evil. What a marvelous characterization from his Creator. So, Satan quickly worked to undo Job's godly way of being.

In the first test, Job loses just about everything imaginable in one blow: his oxen and donkeys and servants, his sheep and camels – even his children and his health. What astounds me is what follows all of that. Job fell to the ground and worshiped God; trusting His sovereignty, without sinning and without blaming God for anything.

After this, God again presented Job as a man of utmost integrity, retaining that great depth and strength of character amidst such loss and turmoil. His own wife and closest friends told him to curse God and die. Job definitely felt sadness, loss, deep pain, and communicated his frustration. He ultimately continued to bless the name of the Lord. God restored Job to a life better than the one he had once known. His possessions were doubled and he was blessed in the latter part of his life even more so than in the earlier part.

The true testament of our worship comes not from a beautifully sung masterpiece of music, nor the feelings we get as the Holy Spirit moves over a room and the anointing is so heavy that we can hardly stand. These may all be components of our worship. But the ultimate testimony is in the position of our hearts in the midst of sadness, loss, unfairness, and all that can come in life.

Maybe it is true that God is more concerned with our character than our comfort, as my pastor often says. Is our initial knee-jerk reaction to tragedies and unfortunate circumstances in life to fall on our knees and worship the Lord in the beauty of His holiness?

Breaking Up Fallow Ground

David M. Edwards

Going through the
motions doesn't
please you; a flawless
performance is nothing
to you. I learned to
worship when my pride
was shattered. Heart-
shattered lives ready
for love don't for a
moment escape God's
notice.

~ David

Have you ever walked on soil when it's below zero? I have; the earth is as hard as a rock around here in the dead of winter. If you have a garden, you know that even after winter wears off the ground is still rigid. Fields are crusted over with the slow-thawing earth.

To date I've never seen a farmer go out in early spring and simply throw seed on top of that crusty soil, go back in his house, and just wait for harvest. A farmer knows that he has to till that fallow soil until it's soft again. Only then is it ready to receive the seeds that will produce a harvest in five or six months.

Sadly, there are many of us who run from church service to church service simply throwing seed on the soil of peoples' lives, thinking it will take root and grow on its own. An entire silo full of seed will do you no good until you have soil that's been broken up and ready to receive it.

"Sow for yourselves righteousness; reap in mercy; break up your fallow ground, for it is time to seek the Lord, till He comes and rains righteousness on you. You have eaten the fruit of lies, because you trusted in your own way, in the multitude of your mighty men." (Hos 10:12-13, NKJV)

Fallow ground is land left uncultivated. The land we're talking about is not soil, but rather the land of our own heart – the field of our soul. How do we know if we have fallow ground? Here are some signs that I've found to be warning signals of hardened ground in the soul: when I don't enjoy worship, when church becomes optional, when I become cynical about other believers and make light of those in the ministry or the message that God has given them, when prayer becomes an option, when I stop giving God my time, talent, and resource, and lastly, when the convicting power of the Holy Spirit is spurned or sloughed off.

You'll notice that breaking up unplowed ground precedes seeking the Lord. Those who want to see the goodness and mercy of the Lord in their lives must come to Him humble, broken, and tender – *soft*! Our fallow ground is broken up by our repenting, breaking up our heart, and coming clean about our priorities that only serve our own interests. Our fallow ground is broken up by our throwing ourselves on the mercy of

God. Our fallow ground is broken up through true worship that pushes past His hands in order to seek His face.

God only uses broken things. I want a direct flow of God in my life. But in order for that to happen, I must sow the seeds of brokenness, tenderness, forgiveness and mercy towards others, seeds of repentance in my own life. Our hearts must burn hot for Jesus!

Break up the surface today. Break up the surface responses that you always give to everyone who asks if things are all right. Break up the facade that you're hiding behind. Seek His face – push aside everything else. Develop and cultivate a familiarity with the presence of God. He's hungry for your worship. He wants to spend time with you. He's just waiting to pour out rain from heaven and water your thirsty, parched soul.

Widow With Two Mites
Lawrence Kimbrough

If worship is an act of attributing to God what already belongs to Him – His glory, His lordship, His sovereignty, His amazing grace – then giving is worship's most practical expression. The ease with which we release our money for no expected return indicates how deeply worship has penetrated our lives. If it can make it to our pocketbooks, it has made it to our hearts.

So when a shawl-covered widow shuffled into the temple one day, feebly fingered the empty corners of her change purse, and silently placed two throw-away coins in the collection box, she unknowingly set a landmark standard of worship for all time.

Her giving, her worship, was complete. Her heart was 100 percent God's.

In one sense, the widow's offering is equivalent to withdrawing every penny from your bank account, selling off all your assets, and writing a check for the entire amount to your church. That's the traditional analogy.

In another sense, though, it requires much more than that to measure the cost of her gift or the size of her faith.

The simple fact that you even have a savings account, or a home, or a car, perhaps a pension plan to liquidate – not to at all minimize the huge impact such a transaction would have on you – still infers that you have a reasonable possibility of rebuilding some sort of life for yourself in your own strength. You have relationships. You have contacts. You have a means of generating income.

This widow had nothing. Nothing going for her. Nothing but an invisible hope that God *"administers justice for the fatherless and the widow, and loves the stranger, giving him food and clothing." (Deut 10:18, NKJV)*

That was it.

We don't know the rest of her story. All we know is that Jesus, who just prior to her arrival had been dressing down Israel's proudest, most well-known "worshipers," knew this widow would be coming by that day, knew her situation, knew her need. With His own eyes, He saw her drop the first coin into the treasury, saw her perhaps hesitate as she held her last penny between her fingers – her last mouthful of food, her last ounce of security – then saw her let it go, saw her eyes close, saw her lips whispering a prayer, saw her faith and worship pushing her farther than she ever thought possible. And in pointing her out to those assembled around Him, He said, *"Truly I say to you, this poor widow put in more than all of them." (Lk 21:4, NASB)*

But I wonder what she was planning to do after leaving the temple that day. Find a shady spot on the street? Melt into the overlooked multitude of the homeless and destitute? Pray for God to take her life? She had taken a chance by putting her last two mites into God's hands. What was her next move going to be?

Nobody knows. But you can sort of guess what happened next. Surely, Jesus had more in mind for her than personifying an object lesson for the ages. You get the feeling He must have gone over to her, asked her why she was crying, listened as she poured her heart out. Imagine her surprise when tears came to His eyes, when He put His strong, comforting arm around her stooped shoulders, when He told her who He was.

She got her two mites worth that day. And then some.

Her Lord Himself had been pleased by her worship. The One whose nature declares that *"he who sows bountifully will also reap bountifully" (2 Cor 9:6, NASB)* had blessed her to her face.

Her 100 percent heart had been 100 percent satisfied.

The Foundation of Worship

Mike Atkins

Surely that which
occupies the total time
and energies of heaven
must be a fitting pattern
for earth.

~ Paul E. Billheimer

Scripture makes it plain that worship is not simply about sounds that come out of my mouth, whether spoken or sung, whether accompanied or a cappella. These can represent the expressions of worship. They can be mediocre or excellent. They can be majestic or simple. But the expression must not be confused with the reality.

Worship is an attitude of heart. Worship happens when I, conscious of the extraordinary grace that has been granted to me by a perfectly holy God, who has borne the weight of my sin, carried my transgressions and sorrows, and burst the bonds of my affliction, come humbly and tremblingly before the throne of the One who offered such an indescribable gift and bow in homage and gratitude.

Perhaps worship is, at its purest, simply the deafening silence of a fallen creature before a perfect Creator. When a heart broken by the weight of sin and the sorrow of the world hears the good news of grace and, like the leper who was healed, runs and falls at the feet of the Master to pour out tears of desperate thanks, true worship has begun.

Without this worshiping heart the finest music in the world, the most skilled musicians, the finest vocalists, become mere noise and entertainment. With this worshiping heart the humblest song, the simplest rhythm, the poorest offering of praise takes the breath of angels away.

When the combination of a worshiping heart and the skillful musician are found together, however, a rapturous expression of Man's devotion to God's glory is experienced. It is, perhaps, the closest thing to heaven that we can know on earth.

It is when these two components are intentionally and deliberately merged together that a worshiping community finds an avenue opened up that allows a steady traffic of grace, healing, mercy, revelation, and love to flow from the throne of God into, and through, the hearts of its people.

- The Foundation of Worship -

Mike Atkins

Once this merger of a worshiping heart and a skillful hand is experienced, it is not soon forgotten. It leaves an imprint of permanent impact on the lives of those who are fortunate enough to be there when it happens. It supersedes the intellect. It overrides man's natural skepticism. It envelops the heart. It reveals God. It heals the wounded places.

Musical skill divorced from this worshiping heart merely tickles the ears, pleases the senses, and entertains the soul. True worship heals the soul, awakens the spirit, and transforms the life.

Most seem to think that the way to arrive at this place is to concentrate on increasing the level of musicality and skill. In fact, the musicality and skill, important as they are, must be under girded by the broken heart, the contrite spirit, and the humbled life. We would do well to devote at least as much time to assuring these attitudes are securely established as by increasing rehearsal time and acquiring new musical skills.

That is not to suggest that musical skill provides no contribution to the experience of real worship, but simply to place it in its proper priority and value assignment. Can true worship happen without significant musical skill? Unequivocally the answer is yes! Can true worship happen without a worshiping heart? Unequivocally the answer is no! Is the best of all possible worlds the combining of a worshiping heart with a disciplined musical ability? Unequivocally the answer is yes!

First the foundation: a worshiping heart. Next the structure: musical skill. Finally the result: God glorified, man transformed.

In Praise of Three-Way Bulbs

Laurie Klein

Don't ask yourself what
the world needs. Ask
yourself what makes you
come alive, and go do
that, because what the
world needs is people who
have come alive.

~ Gil Bailie

Burned out. Coming unscrewed. Amid semi-gloom, the mottled bulb from my reading lamp jingles when shaken, a tinny, useless music. I go to the closet where spare bulbs nest in their cartons of corrugated paper. The manufacturer promises fifty days' worth of continuous light: 1200 hours. Efficient and adjustable, these 3-way bulbs – like believers engaged in the arts – are also fragile. But careful handling yields beauty. Illumination. And light enough for others to see by.

To produce all three levels of light, the directions say, *the bulb should be tightened firmly but not forcibly in the socket. This will ensure all contacts are connected.* Ideally, we serve where our giftings fit best. But even then, life events and people have a way of jamming and even distorting our signals. A pre-rehearsal time-out with God grounds us: we tap into the power Source. *Otherwise,* as the light bulb manufacturers know, *only one filament may light.*

Like my lamp, my commitment as a worshiper encompasses various settings. I think of this as an action trinity: consecration, concentration, and celebration. When this trio works together, heaven turns on the juice and lights up the room.

First click of the switch: *Consecrate.* I surrender my agenda – my time, my preferred teammates or songs or styles. I resolve to follow the Holy Spirit's direction through the designated leader. And why not invert those burdens I'm toting? Instead of bemoaning worry as my besetting sin, I try to view it as power, then redirect it: a yet-to-be-harnessed energy for meditation. Medicine and psychology both teach that ruminating over something disturbing actually reproduces the initial stress in our minds and bodies. By repeating scripture or edifying song lyrics instead, I subvert worry and fear, quieting the soul for gentle, yet deeper connection with God.

Click it again, Sam; setting two: *Concentrate.* I gauge my energy level, be it sub-basement level or off-the-charts elevated. Asking God to be strong in my weakness when I'm down is now second nature. But when happiness peaks my meters, my nervous energy, enthusiastic interrupting, or giddiness can derail a rehearsal. I've done this enough times to know. My exuberance often stems from the pleasure of being with valued teammates again. But I sometimes need to temper that brightness, depending on who I'm with and what they're experiencing. The French writer Collette once wrote of the "supreme elegance of learning to diminish." While I doubt she had in mind John the Baptist's example, the self-decreasing that the life of Jesus might increase within, there are times for godly restraint. Hopefully, I temper my mood if this seems warranted. One way I do this is by breathing prayers throughout rehearsal, as Rick Warren suggests: *"I love You;"* or *"Jesus, You're with me;" "I want to know You;" "Help!"* or a simple *"Thank You."*

Setting three: *Celebrate.* Now that I'm prepared, I want to make each run-through count: not just practice, but worship. Barring laryngitis or injury, in the theater there's no such thing as holding back during rehearsal. A player gives all, every time. Then, like a lamp put through its paces, grace leads us from glory to glory where, as my bulb manufacturers proclaim: *Satisfaction is Guaranteed.*

Corporate celebration is exhilarating, its joys incandescent; offered authentically, it becomes holiness, the amber corona – the lasting glow of fire.

Rediscovering Rest
Lea Collins

Worship is God's
enjoyment of us and our
enjoyment of Him.

~ Graham Kendrick

Western cultures are fighting an epidemic of lethal proportions. The problem is burnout, a condition caused by too much stress unalleviated for too long. Burnout causes emotional and mental problems (such as depression) as well as physical sickness (stress is a contributor to 90% of all modern diseases). Helping people find their "work-life balance" has become a multi-million dollar industry. If left unchecked, burnout does more than just ruin the quality of life. It can actually kill you. In Japan they have a word for it: karoshi – death from overwork.

In the Christian ministerial community, stress and burnout have become one of the biggest issues of the past decade. In the U.S., more than 1500 pastors leave the ministry each month citing pastoral burnout as one of the major reasons. Articles with headlines like "Death by Ministry" and "Holy Burnout" frequent Christian leadership magazines.

In every sector and industry the answer to this problem is the same. The primary reason burnout happens is the lack of its number one cure: **REST.**

It shouldn't take doctors and statistics to remind believers of the importance of rest. The Bible mentions "rest" 469 times. In contrast, "worship" appears only 250 times and "praise" 326 times. Rest is extremely important to God. So important, in fact, that He made a law about it: remember (observe) the Sabbath.

The word "Sabbath" or "Shabbat" comes from the Hebrew root "Shin-Bet-Tav" which means "to cease," "to end," and "to rest." When God instituted the Sabbath in Jewish culture, it was a completely unprecedented social concept. This weekly day off remained an exclusively Jewish "holiday" until the Reformation when Western Europe rebuilt itself with the Ten Commandments as the basis for society and law. Following this tradition, most of us now have two days off each week – Saturday and Sunday. Saturday is usually consumed with the errands

- Rediscovering Rest -
Lea Collins

and house work we don't have time for during the week. And for those of us involved in any kind of ministry, whether full time or as a volunteer, Sunday is anything but a day of rest. Then it's Monday, back to work until Friday. If we're lucky, rest is penciled in for a week of summer vacation each year. Seven days a year is a far cry from the fifty-two God intended. No wonder we're all burned out!

Biblically and traditionally, the Sabbath is about time to reconnect with ourselves, our families and God in a dedicated, unhurried way. It's about taking a quiet, meditative time out to reflect on our life, our week, and the goodness of God. It's about leisurely enjoyment of nature and remembering how much bigger Life is than what we see from behind our desks. It's about letting our families know they are honored, valued, and priceless to us. Not only is it one of our highest forms of worship, but it's also a required form of worship that God Himself ordained *"as an eternal sign"* of our covenant relationship (Ex 31:17, NIV).

Reintegrating the principle of the Sabbath does not require a Pharisaical system that strictly defines how far we can walk or what sort of cup we're allowed to drink from. In the words of Jesus, the Sabbath was made for man – not man for the Sabbath (Mk 2:27). Jesus repeatedly broke the Sabbath rules of His day: healing people, picking food to eat, walking too far. But Jesus always made up for the Sabbath times He missed – in less religious and more natural ways: extended feasts with His friends, disappearing alone into an ocean or mountain setting to spend time enjoying the beauty of creation with His Father. He taught His disciples to do the same. When they got too caught up with ministry, Jesus would come alongside them and say *"Come with me by yourselves to a quiet place and get some rest."* (Mk 6:31, NIV)

If you listen closely, I bet you'll hear Him saying the same thing to you. The more like Jesus we become, the more time we will spend in rest. God rested from His work after six days of creation. Jesus continually needed to stop and refresh Himself with periods of Sabbath. Do we really think we can worship, serve, and live in the fullness and excellence God desires if we don't learn the discipline of rest?

We are called to worship God with the very best we have. When we run out of our best and do not have that to give, our call is to worship God with our rest.

John

Lawrence Kimbrough

To read the apostle John's letters, you wouldn't be surprised to find tear stains on the pages. He talks like a grandfather: how proud he is of them, how much he longs to be with them, how he agonizes over their hurts and warns them to be careful out there. Not exactly what you'd expect from someone known as a Son of Thunder.

But that's what loving God can do in a person's life. And John really loved God.

At first, perhaps, it was fascination. Curiosity. Something different than fishing, for a change. But those eyes – those inviting, penetrating eyes of the Man who met him on the Galilean seashore, the Man who introduced Himself as Jesus of Nazareth – those eyes felt like they could see to the back wall of his soul.

It didn't take much for John to be drawn to Him, to watch His miracles and be wowed by His power, to worship Him as the living answer to centuries of divine prophecy. That was easy.

But it did take a lot to believe that Jesus could love him, that He could listen patiently while John was asking permission to blowtorch an apathetic Samaritan village (Lk 9:51-55) or reserving luxury box seats in the new kingdom (Mk 10:35-40).

That was, until one unforgettable Friday in the eerie midday darkness at the base of a cross, his arms around Mary's shivering, sobbing frame, when John saw love in its rawest, purest form. And suddenly he realized, *"In this is love, not that we loved God, but that He loved us and sent His Son." (1 Jn 4:10, NASB)* As much as he loved his Lord, it was nothing compared to Jesus' love for John.

That love became the core of John's message.

Maybe that's why, though the other Gospel writers chronicled the life of Jesus primarily by recalling facts and reporting stories, John chose to paint a more intimate picture: of feet humbly washed by the One who had created them, of a Shepherd praying passionately for His flock, almost wishing His Father would let Him stay behind to keep an eye on them, to keep their spirits up through the tough times that lay ahead.

John wanted to make sure that the young church of new believers, those who would have to follow without the benefit of walking shoulder to shoulder with Jesus, could see Him through the eyes of one who knew

His voice, recognized His laugh, witnessed His transfigured glory. He hoped that even with Jesus ascended to the Father, they could worship Him *"in spirit and truth." (Jn 4:24, NASB)*

That was the worship John knew. Not worship service worship. But all-the-time worship.

Worship that costs you something. Worship that can stare down the barrel of forced labor on the harsh, forsaken island of Patmos and remain open to God's Revelation.

Worship that's more than saying the right words, but growing and acquiring a right heart – a heart that truly loves other people – because *"Whoever does not practice righteousness is not of God, nor is he who does not love his brother. For this is the message that you heard from the beginning, that we should love one another." (1 Jn 3:10-11, NKJV)*

John's worship motivated right actions, and right actions fueled the authenticity of his worship. It all tied together, keeping him at peace with God and at peace with man, and becoming more like Jesus, even to the point of death. *"The world is passing away, and the lust of it; but he who does the will of God abides forever." (1 Jn 2:17, NKJV)*

And if He's anything like John, He also loves forever.

We Were Made to Worship

Regi & Kimberlee Stone

The most eloquent prayer
is the prayer through
hands that heal and
bless. The highest form of
worship is the worship of
unselfish Christian service.
The greatest form of
praise is the sound of
consecrated feet seeking
out the lost and helpless.

~ Billy Graham

Have you ever noticed someone in church who doesn't participate in worship? Not one word, not one note, not with clapping or raising of their hands. What about the painful experience of sitting in front of someone who sings all the songs without hitting one right note? It can be an agonizing experience either way. Feeling like you have nothing to offer during worship because you cannot perfect the notes or tune is discouraging. It can lead a person to believe that they don't amount to as much in God's eyes as the stellar soloists who take the platform Sunday after Sunday.

Maybe you feel like you don't "do" worship very well. A friend of mine who finds it difficult to raise his hands or sing above a faint whisper in church once told me that he doesn't feel like he does worship well. While I wasn't sure what he meant by that at first, I've come to realize that many people feel the same. Unfortunately, there is a misconception that worship is defined only by singing songs in corporate praise and worship.

Worship is much more than Sunday mornings, or praise choruses, or even hymns! Instead, it is perfected in the every day of our lives. It is more about the attitudes of our hearts and less about our platform skills or our ability to hit a high C in head voice. Worship from us to God happens when we stand in line at the grocery store and say "Thank you, God, for the ability to pay for what's in our basket," and then make the cashier's day by paying her a compliment. It's when we call on the name of Jesus for our sick child because the medicine isn't helping. It's in helping the homeless and wrapping our arms around the lonely.

What's even greater is that worship not only happens from us to God, but its benefits come down from God to us. There are times in our lives when we are at a complete loss for words, void of emotion, and stuck in a chasm of grief or hopelessness. It is difficult, if not impossible sometimes, to find the strength to reach up to God. We need help. We need an intercessor.

A friend tells the story of a woman who slipped into a coma for a few days. When she came to and began talking with her family, someone asked if she remembered anything. All she could recall was that God had been singing a song to her while she was in a deep sleep. I stopped, a bit confused. God was doing the singing? Now *that's* a song and melody I would love to know!

Soon after, I began searching the scriptures for evidence that God would do something as wonderful as that in the middle of this woman's utter helplessness. During my pursuit, I turned to this passage in the Bible:

> *"The Lord your God is with you, he is mighty to save. He will take great delight in you, he will quiet you with his love, he will rejoice over you with singing." (Zeph 3:17, NIV)*

The picture is not an easy one to grasp, but let's attempt to put it into modern terms. God our Father is doing whatever it is that He does in heaven: listening to the innocent prayers of children, hearing us ask for better jobs and more patience, watching over us as we drive across town. The requests and thanksgiving of His children fill His ears like a symphony in a thousand different languages. Yet amidst the waves of sound that float up to Him, there is a still, small sound that makes Him smile. It is you calling out to Him! This time you don't need anything; no emergency, no miracle healing. You're just taking a moment to focus on Him because He's HIM.

From the highest throne in heaven, He looks down and rejoices… over you. He begins to sing. Not just any song, but a divine tune intended just for this moment, and specifically to minister to you. And all because He loves you that much. You know it is Him because there is a warmth that invades your soul, comfort that takes up where there was once hurt, joy that words won't convey, and peace that goes way beyond making sense. There is simply no way for my mind to fathom that song. Oh, what it must sound like!

The next time you think God is saying, "Come on, join Me. Worship Me with your whole heart. Your whole being. With every ounce of who I made you to be." Don't be afraid to ask Him, "But how? I have no talent to sing or play or dance."

He may say something like, "That's not what I want. I want your obedience." He is simply looking for the kind of obedience that says, "Take my finances, my abilities, my children, my home, my prayers. Use them to bless others." It is exactly through those humble offerings that we present our gift of worship. Then, like a singer getting ready for a performance, I can hear Him warming up His vocal chords. Suddenly, without the need for a large choir dressed in fancy robes, a high tech sound system, or a worship team, He bursts into a song Himself!

When we worship, we experience. Those experiences shape who we are and who we become. The next time you find yourself in a time of personal worship through prayer, song, giving, or good deeds, remember that you just made God smile. He takes great delight in you. He rejoices over you. So worship Him.

It's what we were made to do.

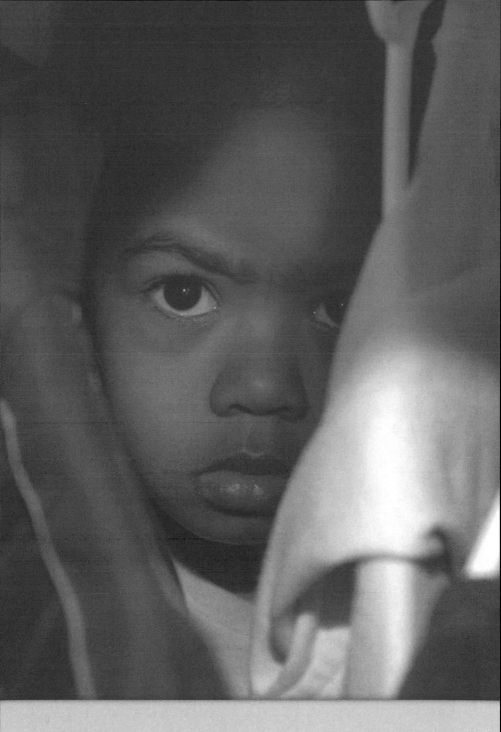

Don't Hide, Be Hidden
Drew Cline

The self is just not a
worthy enough vehicle
to worship.

~ Peter Coyote

When I was a little guy, I remember getting in trouble with my parents, running to my room, and hiding in the closet. It's not like that was the safe haven where no discipline would find me. In fact, it was usually the very place my father would find a trusty belt to remind me of why it's good to be obedient.

The truth is it's our heritage to hide. When we've truly messed up and know it, it's only "natural" to want to remove ourselves from the situation and run to some dark place where the consequences of that action hopefully won't follow.

But they always do. I say it's our heritage because even in the garden, Adam and Eve sinned, heard God walking and calling out to them, and then hid. I think the cause of this desire to run and hide is shame. Shame, by definition, is a negative emotion that combines feelings of dishonor, unworthiness, and embarrassment. Even at a very young age when we're disobedient, we know that our action will most likely bring some act of discipline – and that's the part we hate. We don't usually mind the sin so much; it's more the consequences that cause us to find the nearest closet.

As we grow older, the closet seems to lose its ability to cover and protect us, so we find new places to hide. As adults it's easier for us to hide emotionally, to detach ourselves from the reality of our situation or sin and hide in destructive places. We often retreat to the shelter of our Lazyboy, a good game on television, our work, the Internet. We can hide from reality with a good romance novel, a shopping spree, a soap opera. We can run to the gym; we can "comfort eat." Our families and friends still see us and we may even fool enough people in our churches that they think we're doing just fine, but often our true hearts are lonely, afraid, and hidden in the closet of some dark addiction instead of the transparent solace of our Father's arms.

Psalm 139:23-24 says *"Search me, O God, and know my heart; test me and know my anxious thoughts. See if there is any offensive way in me, and lead me in the way everlasting." (NIV)* To make this your prayer, you've got to be ready to be undone, floored by God's grace, to be completely open to His Spirit, and willing to allow Him to purge you of every wrong thing. As a worshiper, your heart should be seeking God, asking Him to look deep into the reality of who you are, to draw you out of your hiding places into His marvelous light.

Know, however, the wonderful irony of God is that we don't have to hide from God when we feel guilty or shameful, but instead let Him be our hiding place. Let His grace be the first place we run *to*, not from. Our nature is to run away from God when we've sinned, but through Jesus, God has given us a new life and a new direction. We may now find our hiding place in God and come boldly before Him.

What exactly in your life are you hiding from God, from your spouse, or from the truth of scripture? There is healing, and hope, and help if we'll just not run away from God to hide but instead, to hide in the shadow of His wing. Let Jesus be your hiding place.

Modern Man and Ancient Songs
Dan Scott

The whole person, with
all his senses, with
both mind and body,
needs to be involved
in genuine worship.

~ Jerry Kerns

Preachers used to tell a lot of stories in the pre-television days when I was a little boy. Whether they were all true or not, I can't say – but they were interesting! I have long forgotten what the stories were supposed to illustrate but I have remembered the stories themselves, which explains, I suppose, why Jesus used story telling almost exclusively as a way to teach.

One story in particular that has stuck with me was about a boy named Johnny. (Now that I recall, all the stories were about Johnny, or Suzy, who must have been Johnny's sister.) This Johnny was marching in a parade but his steps were out of sync. When the parade organizers investigated, they discovered that Johnny was wearing an ear phone connected to a transistor radio. What he had been doing was keeping perfect time with the music he was listening to, which is also what caused him to be out of step with the music of the band in which he was marching.

Christians are often like Johnny. The parade around us is moving. Our fellow citizens seem to be moving in harmony with one another but we often find ourselves out of step with them. This is because we are listening to another sort of music. I think that ancient peoples probably knew more about this music than we moderns do. I believe that even nature hears that music and moves – the best that it can in its fallen state – to the rhythm it hears from another place and another time. That music, so out of step with our age, is the timeless song the writer had in mind when he invited us to "come join the chorus, the mighty, mighty chorus, which the morning stars began." It is a music many of our countrymen search for their entire lives. It is a music that awakens one from the evil spell which tries to shut our ears to the song of songs.

The first step toward learning to hear the timeless music is to understand that nothing that is true is ever new. There are new applications of truth. There are new discoveries and rediscoveries. But all that is really true and all that is truly valuable are simple things which get repeated from age to age and from culture to culture. A man or woman in search of wisdom will sooner or later be amused to discover that Grandma's old sayings were simply the way the world works. A stitch in time still saves nine and a soft answer still turns away wrath.

- Modern Man and Ancient Songs -

Dan Scott

In every age the great men and women have been those who rediscovered timeless truths. Beethoven wrote the music to which we sing the lyrics of "Joyful, Joyful, We Adore Thee." (He would probably be appalled at how we play it now, but that would be his problem!) So if the music rings and resonates with us, it is because Beethoven echoed an ageless melody that fits perfectly into a space within our hearts made specifically to receive it.

The song fits. After Beethoven, a hymn writer discovered just the right words to fit into the space the music made for a timeless message. So when he wrote "Come join the chorus, the mighty, mighty chorus, which the morning stars began," he was simply inviting yet another generation to participate in the timeless expression of worship in the heavenlies.

When Job got out of sorts with God and started ranting about how the world wasn't made right, God shouted back these words to His friend.

> *"Then the LORD answered Job out of the whirlwind, and said,*
> *'Who is this that darkeneth counsel*
> * by words without knowledge?*
> *Gird up now thy loins like a man;*
> * for I will demand of thee, and answer thou me.*
> *Where wast thou when I laid*
> * the foundations of the earth?*
> * declare, if thou hast understanding.*
> *Who hath laid the measures thereof, if thou knowest?*
> * or who hath stretched the line upon it?*
> *Whereupon are the foundations thereof fastened?*
> * or who laid the corner stone thereof;*
> *When the morning stars sang together,*
> * and all the sons of God shouted for joy?'"*

(Job 38:1-7, KJV)

That's what moved Job to worship. That's what always moves all of us to worship. If we can only hear, even for a few seconds, the timeless song, our feet will pick up the beat and they will turn toward a city not made with hands.

And *that* is what worship is for.

Just Let Go
Gordon Mularski

Are you tired?
Worn out?
Burned out on religion?

Come to me.
Get away with me and you'll
recover your life. I'll show
you how to take a real rest.
Walk with me and work with
me - watch how I do it. Learn
the unforced rhythms of
grace.
I won't lay anything heavy or
ill-fitting on you.

Keep company with me.
You'll learn to live freely and
lightly.

~ Jesus

She stands beside a lake in the mountains, all ponytails and smiles. Her nine year old frame looks microscopic against the rugged backdrop. In her hand she holds a rope connected to the tallest pine tree you have ever seen.

"I'm gonna do it, Daddy," echoes her voice across the lake. Her father is positioned right about where he thinks she will enter the water. He feels for her as she looks with apprehension at the water below. "You can do it!" he calls to her.

She grips the rope a little tighter. Her hands begin to sweat. Her heart begins to beat a little faster. Her mind is racing. She knows this could be dangerous, but she also knows this could be the ride of her life. The question is: *will she give it a try?*

Inside we root for the little girl. We would encourage the brave little soul that climbed up the mountainside with phrases like, "You can do it" or "Just try it once!" We hate to see anyone frozen by fear and robbed of an experience that they will remember forever.

The sad truth is that it happens every Sunday when the first note is played and the frozen chosen sit back and "wait" for the teaching. They miss the experience of worship and focus solely on the academic. They just want to sit and be taught. They have come to church for their benefit and not for His. They forget that they are in His house and have forgotten how much they have already been given. Knowledge that refuses passion quickly turns into religion; religion shapes up the outside and kills what is on the inside. (Matt 23:27-28)

Why do we stand on the edge of opportunity and fear where the ride of true worship may take us? Who told us that expressive worship was wrong? Doesn't passion spring from a love relationship? Who benefits from you keeping your godly passion under "proper" control? Your passion in worship is an expression of the abundant life you have been given in Christ. To contain your expression of worship means to compromise your gift to your King. David would not compromise his expression of worship and was criticized by those closest to him. His expression made his wife uncomfortable, but the expression of his heart is what made him special to God.

- Just Let Go -
Gordon Mularski

Scripture states that as *"we are receiving a kingdom that cannot be shaken, let us be thankful, and so worship God acceptably with reverence and awe, for our 'God is a consuming fire.'"* (Heb 12:28-29, NIV) God is not a spark that gets a fire going. God is not a candle that brings some light to a room. God is a consuming fire. A consuming fire takes over whatever it touches. The thought of that can be initially scary because it means that we have in a sense lost control.

This could be dangerous.

This could also be the wildest and most rewarding ride you have ever been on.

Remember the little girl on the rope swing? She never gave it a try. She tried to slide down the hill and play it safe. She ended up cut, bruised, and defeated. The worst part of the story is that she missed the ride.

Worship is a ride. It is an action. It is an expression. It is also at times uncomfortable, but it is never without reward.

The little girl refused a memorable ride.

Will you?

Experiencing worship requires action.

You could just read this book, (possibly) feel warm and inspired, set it back down and not do anything differently. But that's not the point. The perspectives in this book are meant to be discussed, evaluated, debated, marked up with your thoughts and ideas, then taken to action.

We have listed two "experiments" for each article in the book. The suggested "experiments" allow for a combination of reflection, discussion, and experience. They are designed for a small group setting to be experienced in community with other people who are working through this book. Most will work with children as well as adults (with some slight language contextualization for young audiences).

Most of these require preparation or planning; you won't be able to just show up and work through them on your first read-through. They are mostly inexpensive and are very participatory.

Better still, these are just suggestions to get you going. They aren't formulas or exclusive ways to hammer home the truth. Each group will be as different as each person who is in it. We've left blank space under each of our suggestions for you to write in your own ideas and make notes of what you actually did – what did and didn't work. If you're a leader or facilitator, this will make it easier for you the next time you work through this with a group (we know from experience how frustrating it is to forget that brilliant thing you did last time and have no idea what folder or safe place is keeping your notes). However you proceed as a group, allow some undirected time for each person to share and process their thoughts after reading the article before going in a particular direction as a group.

So test these out, come up with your own, and be sure to stop by www. experienceworship.com to tell us about your experiences and ideas. We're always taking suggestions for practical, not-*just*-musical ways to experience worship!

Leaders & Facilitators: Don't forget that you can purchase this entire book or individual articles (with their Worship in Action points) in downloadable format at www.experienceworship.com . Unlike the printed book, the downloadable versions come with reproducible copyright permissions which enable you to make as many copies as you need for your group. This is a legal, cost effective alternative for using this book (or single articles) in a group without everyone purchasing their own copy – and it spares you 30 minutes at the copy machine each week.

1 Experiencing Worship

REFLECT What in your life makes you feel as if God made you to do that thing? Are you creative? Good at leading people? Do you love to run?

DISCUSS What are some practical ways you can use those natural expressions of your skills and interests – your life – as acts of worship? How can you implement them this week?

2 Why Do We Worship?

DISCUSS Transformation. What kinds of animals start in one form and become another? What does that tell us about God? What might that tell us about ourselves?

EXPERIENCE Draw a picture (stick figures are fine) of the person you were before you met Jesus (or for those who met Jesus when they were young, before you decided to follow Him fully with the rest of your life). Then draw a picture about the person you are now. Can you see a change?

3 Lift Your Eyes

REFLECT Take honest stock of your life, right now. How do you feel? How is your life affecting your feelings? Is there anything you can specifically identify in God's nature that can bring you comfort/joy/encouragement?

EXPERIENCE Write a psalm to God which talks about the process and provides answers to the questions above. Take a risk and be vulnerable: read it aloud and discuss how writing the words affected you, what the process made you think and feel.

4 Abraham

REFLECT What impossible promises – things that cannot possibly happen without God – does God give us in the Bible? What impossible promises has He given you personally?

DISCUSS If belief begins with curiosity and faith comes from living out belief, where are you on your journey of faith? Is it easy or hard for you to believe that God will do as He says?

5 The Heart of Worship

REFLECT What areas in your life do you need to sacrifice? Do you need to confess your sins? Offer or ask for forgiveness? Cry out to God because you're experiencing a lot of difficulties? Give an impassioned exaltation (praise) to God for the things He has done?

EXPERIENCE If anyone is in need of forgiveness for sin, give them opportunity to repent, receive forgiveness from God, hear that forgiveness affirmed by the believers they are with, and then passionately thank God for the grace He has given. Discuss what it means to worship God when you know how much it has cost you. End with communion.

6 Diving In

REFLECT Take a moment and think about how big God is. Really think about what it actually means to relate to Him as a child. Ask Him to help you come to Him with simple faith.

EXPERIENCE With finger-paint, paint what the hugeness of God makes you feel like. It can be a picture or just shapes, lines, and colors. When everyone is done, have show and tell time.

7 Holy Rain

DISCUSS What does it mean to you that God is everywhere? How would it change your worship if He was physically there and you could see Him watching you?

EXPERIENCE Take a few familiar songs of worship and just say the words out loud. Go around the room and put the thought behind the lyrics in your own words, restating them from your own perspective with words you use when you're really being yourself.

8 Joseph

REFLECT Think about the times when your life has been the most difficult. How have those experiences affected the way you come to God?

EXPERIENCE Put together a puzzle. Have everyone work together on a large puzzle or several small puzzles, but be sure you are working together (everyone doesn't get their own puzzle!). As you are working, tell stories about times in your life that were really difficult, and how those experiences made you who you are.

9 The Size of Our God & The Size of Our Worship

EXPERIENCE Plan a field trip. Go to a park, the beach, the mountains, a zoo, botanical gardens – wherever you can go and interact with God's creation.

REFLECT Think about what kind of God had to make everything. Can you contain Him? If this huge God were really, visibly present right where you are, how would it affect you?

10 Circle of the Broken

EXPERIENCE Have everyone bring a candle. Go around the room and give prayer requests. Hold hands and pray that God will help you all trust in His ability and desire to meet your needs. Then pray for each person individually. After you pray for someone, have them light their candle. When you have prayed for each person, turn out the lights and sit in the candlelight for some quiet reflection time.

REFLECT After prayer, take a moment of silence in the candlelight and think about all the characteristics of God you can bring to mind. Think about how each of us adds to the Body of Christ, as every lit candle adds to the light in the room.

11 Friend of God

EXPERIENCE Write a letter to a close friend. As you write, think of how well you know this person. Tell them what makes them important to you.

DISCUSS What does it mean to be God's friend? How does being His friend affect you? How does this relationship with God affect our other relationships?

12 Moses

REFLECT What things in your life, personality, or character do you need God's help to overcome?

DISCUSS Do your own limitations make it hard for you to understand God's character? For example, if it's hard for you to trust, how hard is it to base real life decisions on God being trustworthy and really coming through for you? Discuss how God often uses people who are unqualified. What does this say about His character?

13 Where Worship Begins

EXPERIENCE Plant a seed with your hands. Make sure you take time to feel your fingers in the dirt and get some stuck underneath your fingernails. Think about the process of growth and how dirty the beginnings of things often are. As you scrub your hands, think about how good it feels to be clean after getting dirty.

DISCUSS Briefly share the story about how you met Jesus with your group. Talk about all of the different ways beginnings can come.

14 Thirty Second Blessing

EXPERIENCE / DISCUSS Throw a party to celebrate today. Blow up balloons. Write on cards or small sheets of paper what you each are thankful for, and put them in a basket. Have a cake (or whatever makes you feel festive) with a candle on it for each person. After each person takes a card from the basket and reads the thanks out loud, blow out the candles and enjoy the yummy treat.

15 The Responsibility of Worship

REFLECT Is your worship more about you, or Jesus? Is it hard for you to "feel" the presence of God when you don't like the music?

DISCUSS Read a psalm together. Discuss what the author might have been experiencing when the psalm was written, and how God is worshiped through the psalm. What aspect of God is being worshiped?

16 Gideon

REFLECT Are you a skeptic? Why? Where is that a strength in your life and where is it a weakness? Does it get in the way of your relationship with God?

EXPERIENCE Read the story of Gideon and/or discuss the life of C.S. Lewis. How does God use skeptics? Talk about your questions and needs.

17 What's Mine is Mine

EXPERIENCE Have your group meet in a restaurant or a coffee shop instead of meeting at your normal location. Have everyone bring an offering – whatever they are able to bring – to use as a tip for the server or barista, whether they order anything or not, regardless of the quality of service. If anyone can't afford to do this, have someone volunteer to bring extra.

DISCUSS Talk about what it means to serve and how service relates to sacrifice. Have you ever had to sacrifice anything to follow God?

18 Repairing the Altar

DISCUSS Read Revelation 2:1-5. Talk about the difference between looking like we're worshiping and really worshiping from the deepest parts of our hearts and minds. How can we practice authentic worship? What tools do we have to "repair our altar?" What tools do we need?

REFLECT Pray silently for God to help you worship Him honestly. Think about the things you have focused on instead of Him, and ask Him to help you change your focus.

19 The Anointing

EXPERIENCE Pour some olive oil into two smalls bowls. Send one bowl around to touch the oil and smell it. Send another one around to dip some bread in and then eat it (perhaps with some freshly cracked pepper).

DISCUSS If the Holy Spirit is the anointing, what does that actually mean to us? How do we interact with the Holy Spirit? How does the Holy Spirit affect us? What does it mean that we are "set apart?"

20 David

EXPERIENCE David loved the outdoors – so take the group outside. Play a game (anything works) and when it's over, sing songs of worship while you're outside – before you cool down or clean up or compose yourself after the game.

DISCUSS How do the experiential acts of worship that characterized David compare to our worship? What does it mean to experience worship?

21 Tears of Joy

EXPERIENCE Watch a funny movie – or at least a long segment of one.

DISCUSS What is so freeing about laughter? Can you force a laugh and make it sound authentic? How do we know when laughter is faked? How can we make our worship a natural, joyful response to God?

22 Communion

EXPERIENCE Make a spiritual family tree. Put as many people as you can think of who have influenced your faith on it, along with a little of what you know of their background. Step back and look at where you come from. Then add the people who you influence – both peers and people you might lead or mentor.

REFLECT Think about the full nature of communion and the Body of Christ.

23 Holy is Your Name

DISCUSS What gifts have you received that really meant a lot to you? What does it mean to you when someone gives you a "perfect gift?" Have you ever given someone a gift that meant a lot to them? If you could give God something just because you knew He enjoyed it and not because you felt obligated to, what would it be?

REFLECT How can you give God your gifts? Don't just think vaguely or conceptually. How can you actually give God your gifts? What can you give Him this week?

24 Solomon

EXPERIENCE Turn all of the noise off – the phones, the TV, the music, anything in the background. Unplug any loud or buzzing appliances; take the batteries out of that ticking clock. Sit with everyone in silence for at least five minutes. Think about God for as long as you can.

DISCUSS What did your mind go to when you got distracted? Think about our culture. What gets in the way of worshiping God? How do we learn to let worshiping God be its own reward? What would that look like if it became prevalent in the Body of Christ?

25 Yielded Instruments

DISCUSS How can you worship outside of singing songs? What can you do to regularly participate in worship that is expressed through caring for "the least of these" as a group as well as on your own?

EXPERIENCE Perform an act of service: collect donations for a food bank, adopt a low-income family for the holidays, volunteer at a soup kitchen or with a Habitat for Humanity project.

26 Room 313

EXPERIENCE Have a potluck dinner. If anyone in your group can't bring something, have someone volunteer to bring extra. End the meal with communion.

DISCUSS As everyone is eating, discuss what it means for our bodies to be a temple or sanctuary. Just as everyone brought something different to the meal, discuss what it looks like in the Body of Christ when we join together with what we each bring. When we are all eating food that everyone has brought, does it matter who brought more? Does it matter who brought less?

27 A Perfect Heart

REFLECT Do you or does someone you know lack hope? Why do you think that is? Is there anything about God's nature that could give hope to that situation?
EXPERIENCE What is it about God that makes you want to sing? Say one thing you can think of out loud, and address it directly to Him. Have someone write down everyone's phrases and then read them together. What kind of song would that be?

28 Elijah

REFLECT What does it feel like when God convicts you? How do you respond?
DISCUSS Is there anyone in your life who confronts you consistently? How does that make you feel? How does God's conviction compare to our interpersonal confrontation?

29 Reasonable Worship

DISCUSS What does it look like to worship God with our minds? What gets in the way of being able to worship God with our thoughts and our intellect as well as with our emotions and our songs?

EXPERIENCE Pick one thing in your life that you've been putting off and do it. Note how following through what you thought you should do with a choice to get it done and then the action of doing it affected the way you feel. When you're done, call someone from your group and tell them how it went.

30 Only the Dance

REFLECT What experiences in your life make you feel like you're going "three steps forward, one step back?" Do you feel discouraged about it?

DISCUSS What are you thankful for? Talk about what there is to be thankful for even when life is difficult, and what difficulties there are even when life is good. How do we learn to worship regardless of circumstances?

31 The Fourth Man

DISCUSS Have you ever faced a choice that meant you had to give something up to obey God or keep it and disobey Him? Did God help you with that choice? Did you make the "right" choice?

EXPERIENCE Consider where you can provide support to people who are struggling and need to know they're not alone. As a group, visit a nursing home, read at a children's hospital, feed the homeless, hold babies at an orphanage – whatever you do, be sure you find people who are generally forgotten and keep them company.

32 Nehemiah

REFLECT What relationships in your life need to be rebuilt? Do you feel like you share God's heart for that situation? How would God have you act: repent for your actions; pray for that relationship; serve that person? How might God have you go about rebuilding and repairing those broken areas?

EXPERIENCE Volunteer to help a low-income family or person with work on their home. As a group, raise funds for the project, then help out with the labor.

33 Never Give Up

DISCUSS What things in your life are you struggling to be patient with? Share your experiences of learning to be patient with the people in your life, with difficult situations, and with God.

EXPERIENCE Take a hike or a long walk. In any group there will be a wide variety of athletic ability, so pick a route that isn't too hard and have the ones who are used to exercise carry extra water and watch out for those who are less athletic. As you walk, discuss patience. (And don't forget emergency supplies!)

34 Overwhelmed?

DISCUSS What things in your life are overwhelming? Can you remember when God met your needs in the past? How does that memory affect you?

EXPERIENCE Figure out practical ways to help the people in the group deal with the things that are currently overwhelming them. Then help them.

35 When the Pressure's On...WORSHIP

EXPERIENCE Have the group memorize a list of five items – then don't mention it again. Go outside, have each person attempt to walk down the driveway or through the parking lot while balancing a hard-boiled egg on a small plastic spoon. When everyone gets done trying, see who remembers the list.

DISCUSS How do distractions affect our ability to apply what we know? How does this relate to worry? Could we reverse the effect, and have worship make us forget our worry? How?

36 Simeon

DISCUSS Have you ever waited a long time for God to fulfill a promise? Are you still waiting? What does God give us to help us be patient?

EXPERIENCE As you are talking, have a beautiful dessert in the middle of the room that no one is allowed to eat until the end. Have two bowls out, one filled with dried beans. Every time someone loses their train of thought or notices they've stopped listening because they're thinking about the dessert, they have to put a bean into the empty bowl. At the end of your discussion time when you are about to eat the dessert, compare the bowls. Which one is more full? What does that say about focus? What does that say about distraction?

37 Trust and Obey

DISCUSS What kind of circumstances make it hard for you to trust Jesus?

EXPERIENCE Print out full-color pictures of different skies with different lighting levels and weather patterns and cloud formations. Lay those out on the floor or on a table and look through them as a group. Which one is your favorite? Why? How does it reflect your relationship with Jesus?

38 Simple

REFLECT Do you overcomplicate your worship? If so, why is that? When did it start? How can you integrate more simplicity into your worship?

EXPERIENCE With a variety of mediums available (paint, pencil, crayon, charcoal, clay, small "building" things, etc.), have everyone express God's simplicity through an artistic creation. Talk about worship as an act which can come in forms other than music.

39 Call Upon the Name of the Lord

REFLECT Do you come to God boldly, knowing that you belong there because of Jesus, or are you timid when you approach God?

DISCUSS What kinds of things does the Bible say we should do in the name of Jesus? What does it mean to be an ambassador of Jesus? How should that knowledge change our worship?

40 John the Baptist

DISCUSS How hard would it be for you to have John the Baptist's job? Why do you think God sent someone to live such a difficult life in order to pave the way for Jesus? Have difficulties in your life ever paved the way for Jesus to come to you?

EXPERIENCE Write about a time when God used difficulties to make way for Jesus to move in your life. Read the stories out loud. End with a time of verbal thanks to God.

41 Why We Worship

DISCUSS What is God like? What are some of His character traits? (It's helpful to write these down.) Do you see any of these attributes in your own life? Were they there before you met Jesus?

EXPERIENCE Write down all of your blessings on individual small pieces of paper. Put everyone's in a bowl or basket. Have someone count them. Thank God for allowing so many blessings in your group.

42 Yet Will I Hope in Him

REFLECT Is it easy for you to worship God when bad things happen? Or is it easier to forget what God is like in those times?

DISCUSS Read through the last few chapters of Job. What does God say we should remember when life is really difficult? How hard or easy is that for you? How does His command to worship Him through every circumstance make you feel?

43 Breaking Up Fallow Ground

DISCUSS Are you soft ground or hard ground? What has God done in your life to make it easier for you to receive what He gives you? What areas are still too hard to receive from God?

EXPERIENCE As you're discussing, play with modeling clay. Notice how difficult it is to mold it when you first begin. As you mold it and shape it, think about how you are molded and shaped. What happens when clay dries out?

44 Widow with Two Mites

DISCUSS Has anyone ever given to you when you knew they didn't have much to give? How did that make you feel? Have you ever given to God when you felt you had nothing?

EXPERIENCE Adopt a low-income family for a holiday, or just a random day. Bring them food and toys for the kids. Spend the day playing with the family and end with a festive meal together.

45 The Foundation of Worship
DISCUSS What does discipline have to do with worship?
EXPERIENCE Before the group starts, choose 1 or 2 hymns that will not be overly familiar to your group and have deep, thoughtful lyrics. Print them out so each person has their own sheet. Allow time for each person to quietly read through the lyrics several times on their own, letting the truth of the words really sink in. Then sing them together.

46 In Praise of Three Way Bulbs
REFLECT Do you feel burned out? Take some time to write out to God what makes you feel burned out.
EXPERIENCE As a group, pray together and give God whatever burdens anyone is carrying. Ask Him to help you focus on Jesus. Then celebrate Him as a group. Celebration can come in many ways: you can sing a song, or paint, or tell the things you are thankful for – just be sure the expression is natural to your group.

47 Rediscovering Rest

DISCUSS Why did God give us the Sabbath? Can anyone remember the last time they were awake and resting from all forms of work – yard work and housework count! How can we add Sabbath times into our lives? What can you start doing this week? Make a commitment together, pray, and hold each other accountable to your commitments for the next 3 weeks.

EXPERIENCE Send everyone home to rest and spend unexpected time with their loved ones. No working allowed!

48 John

REFLECT What does it mean to truly love?

EXPERIENCE Spend the evening in the park giving away something practical to whoever needs it (like bottles of water or single-ride bus passes). When you give the gift to a stranger, think about how God loved us before we loved Him and try to see God's heart for the people you talk to. Make sure and go out of your way to give to people you wouldn't normally talk to.

49 We Were Made to Worship

EXPERIENCE Think about all of the talents and abilities you have. Ask God to show you what you can give Him as an offering. Write down what you think that God has given you that you can give Him as worship, and share it with the group.

DISCUSS How many different ways do you see God using people in your group in worship? Is it easier to relate to God when you think about the act of worship as more than music or singing? What kind of song would you want God to sing over you?

50 Don't Hide, Be Hidden

DISCUSS Do you hide from God when you feel ashamed? What do you depend on when you don't feel you can go to God? What would it look like if, as a body, we went to God regardless of our own sense of inadequacy?

EXPERIENCE Take time for confession. This doesn't have to be dramatic – it's quite simple. Just confess to each other the things you are currently ashamed of, ask God to forgive you, and receive His forgiveness. After confession, consider how you feel about going to God now.

51 Modern Man and Ancient Songs

REFLECT Do you connect to the "ancient song" the author referenced? Think about some times in your life when you felt connected with God and really realized how huge and timeless His plans are.

DISCUSS Read an old hymn or prayer. Talk about the words, what they mean, and the outlook of the writer towards God. Can you relate to their expression to God?

52 Just Let Go

REFLECT Have you ever missed out on an opportunity because you were afraid to take a risk?

EXPERIENCE Talk to one another about things you believe that God wants you to do but you're afraid to try. Pray with each other for encouragement, and then talk about what action you are going to take. When you leave, begin applying your plan. Hold each other accountable to the process.

Appendix 2:
Author Bios

Ken Abraham

Ken Abraham is a New York Times best-selling author, known around the world for his collaborations with popular celebrities and high-profile public figures such as former U.S. Attorney General John Ashcroft; Senator Bob Dole; Pastor Joel Osteen; actor Chuck Norris; Neil Clark Warren, founder of e-Harmony.com; ASCAP's Gospel songwriter of the century, Bill Gaither. Ken's latest book, "*Threat to Justice*," the second in a three book fiction series written with Chuck Norris, is now available. You can read more about Ken at Penguin Group's website: us.penguingroup.com/nf/Author/AuthorPage/0,,0_1000060654,00. html or http://preview.tinyurl.com/585qbh.

Mike Atkins

Mike Atkins has traveled extensively as a guest lecturer with Youth With A Mission and has authored the book "*Church of the Nations: Becoming a First Century Church in a 21st Century World.*" He is an anointed worshiper and gifted teacher whose inspiring style of communication has led him before a variety of audiences, including China, Korea, Europe, Scandinavia, Great Britain, Africa, India, Central America, the Caribbean, and Israel. He is Senior Pastor of the Jackson Hole Christian Center (www.jhchristiancenter.org) in Jackson Hole, Wyoming. JHCC is a church with a diverse congregation reaching a unique population of global travelers from around the world. Mike is also the founder of River Crossing: a unique, developing outreach venue that utilizes music and performing arts to impact the millions of tourists who pass through Jackson Hole. Mike and his wife Patty have three daughters: Micah, Rebekah and Sarah.

Drew Cline

Since childhood, music has been a major part of Drew's life. A passionate songwriter with a pastor's heart, Drew has worked on projects or performed live with such artists as Third Day, Todd Agnew, Dolly Parton, Sandi Patty, Don Moen, Gaither Vocal Band, and many others. He has recorded numerous commercial projects for NBC's "The Today Show," CMT, HGTV, Kohl's, Chevrolet, Ford, Yamaha, NHL Hockey Team "Roanoke Express," as well as countless publishing demos and performance soundtracks. In 2006 Drew became lead vocalist for the Dove Award winning and Grammy nominated group NewSong. Drew and Lori, his beautiful wife, are committed to their church family at Ecclesia in Franklin, TN where Drew served as worship pastor before going on the road with NewSong. For more about Drew, visit www.drewcline.com.

Lea Collins

Lea loves words. She has been talking in complete sentences since she was 11 months old. As a 2 year old, she once pointed her finger at a Buddha statue in front of a Chinese restaurant and loudly proclaimed, "Behold! A graven image!" As a grown up, Lea's propensity for language got her into client managing/copywriting at abrasiveInk, a Nashville-based branding firm, and directing The Starving Artist Venture. She loves writing, discipleship, almost anything in print, and gets really antsy if she stays in one place for too long. Her husband Andrew keeps up with her remarkably well and makes her happier than anyone else in the world. You can contact her through www.abrasiveink.com or www.StarvingArtistVenture.org.

Dr. David Cooper

Dr. David Cooper serves as senior pastor of Mount Paran Church in Atlanta. He is an author of such books as *"Get A Grip: Facing Life's Toughest Challenges"* and *"Timeless Truths in Changing Times."* He is a songwriter and musician, as well as a professor in counseling at Psychological Studies Institute in Atlanta. You can hear his teaching at www.mountparan.com.

David M. Edwards

David M. Edwards is a teacher, writer, and pastor whose music and teaching ministry have taken him all over the world. David's recent book, *"Worship 365: The Power of a Worshiping Life"* (Broadman & Holman, 2006), is based on his "Power to Worship Encounter" seminars, which help worshipers experience God's presence. To find out more about David's music, books, and ministry, visit www.davidmedwards.com.

Jeff Ferguson

Jeff Ferguson is a songwriter, gospel singer, and minister. As a songwriter, Jeff's music has been recorded over 800 times and nominated for numerous Grammy, Dove and Stellar awards. Jeff lives in Nashville, Tennessee with his daughter, Gabrielle. You can visit Jeff online at www.jeffferguson.com.

Audra Almond-Harvey

Audra Almond-Harvey is an artist, writer, poet, dancer, and pastor at The Anchor Fellowship in Nashville, TN. She loves teaching people to recognize the presence of God as an active force in their lives and often learns what does or doesn't work from her six year old son Selah who likes discussing the character of God while practicing his Jedi moves. In her day jobs Audra doubles as the executive director of abrasiveMedia, an artist focused nonprofit organization, and the artistic director at abrasiveInk, a Nashville-based branding firm. In her occasional free time she enjoys cooking, reading, and giving of her opinions to anyone who will sit and listen. You'll find Audra at www.abrasiveMedia.org and www.abrasiveink.com.

Mark Hodge

Since graduating from Trevecca Nazarene University in 1984, Mark Hodge has provided worship leadership at various churches, including Calvary Church in Cordova, Tennessee where he has served as Pastor of Worship & Arts since 2003. He lives in Cordova with his wife Cindy and their children Taylor and Cameron. You can reach him through www.memphiscalvary.org.

Dallas Holm

Dallas Holm is a long time veteran of Christian music. He has performed over 3,000 concerts in the United States as well as in many countries abroad. Coupled with thirty-five recordings with sales in the millions, number one songs, gold records, a Grammy nomination and multiple Dove awards, as well as an endless list of other awards and achievements, this makes Holm's resume read like a *Who's Who* in a Christian Music Hall of Fame. You can learn more about him at: www.dallasholm.org.

Lawrence Kimbrough

Lawrence Kimbrough is a best-selling devotional and inspirational writer as well as an editor with B&H Publishing Group. He and his wife, Kim, have two daughters (who are getting way too grown up) and make their home just outside of Nashville, Tennessee.

Laurie Klein

An award-winning writer, educator, and performer, Laurie Klein is widely published in journals, anthologies, music resources and recordings. Currently, she's completing a spiritual memoir about her classic chorus, "I Love You, Lord." She works as consulting editor at *Rock & Sling: A Journal of Literature, Art and Faith*. You can contact her through www.rockandsling.org.

Greg Long

Greg Long is a solo artist and a member of the band Avalon. Greg's musical career has produced number one singles, six additional top 10 hits, an ASCAP Award, and two Dove Award nominations. Greg is married to fellow Avalon band member Janna Long. They have two daughters: Lillian and Julia. You can learn more about Greg at www.greglong.com.

Babbie Mason

Babbie Mason is a favorite voice among Christian music recording artists. She is a two-time Dove Award winner and a veteran Christian singer, songwriter, speaker and author. A devoted wife and mother, she and her husband Charles make their home in metro Atlanta. For more information about Babbie and her ministry, visit www.babbie.com.

Reba Rambo-McGuire

Reba Rambo-McGuire, born to Gospel music legends Buck & Dottie Rambo, is an award-winning singer, songwriter, recording artist, author, minister, and pastor. Her albums have sold millions and her songs have been performed by many artists. Reba's recordings have garnered both Grammy and Dove awards; she was inducted into the Gospel Music Hall of Fame in 2001.She lives in Nashville with her husband Dony where they pastor The River at Music City, a church they pioneered several years ago. You can find Reba online at www.theriveratmusiccity.com/.

Gordon Mularski

Gordon Mularski is the Lead Pastor of Treasure Coast Community Church in Jensen Beach, Florida. His passion for life-change motivates him in the ministry of a very active and growing church. He has been married for 17 years and is the proud father of two incredible children. For more information about Gordon and his church, visit www.tc3.org.

Caleb Quaye

Caleb Quaye was born and raised in London, England. During the late sixties and seventies, he was a well known studio musician, Elton John's guitarist for ten years, and also worked with such rock legends as Mick Jagger, Pete Townsend, and Paul McCartney. Now, Caleb is the National Worship Director for the Foursquare denomination and ministers all over the United States and Europe; he also serves as adjunct faculty at LIFE Pacific College in San Dimas California, teaching music and worship leadership. You can learn more about him at www.calebquaye.com.

Harlan Rogers

Harlan Rogers is a jazz musician who has been in the music industry for over forty years. He has worked for many artists, both in live performances and recordings. Some of these artists include Andrae Crouch, The Winans, Danniebelle Hall, the jazz-fusion group Koinonia, Kirk Whalum, Kelly Willard, Debby Boone, Johnny Rivers, Ricky Skaggs, and many others. As a composer, his songs have been recorded by various artists and his credits include writing music for television shows such as *Amen* and *Dear John*. He has also written worship songs for Maranatha Music including Praise 18, 19 and 20.Harlan has started various blogs online as a means of expressing his thoughts and views.

Dan Scott

Dan Scott is senior pastor of Christ Church in Nashville Tennessee. He holds a B.A. degree in History/Sociology, a Masters of Humanities, a Masters in Psychology, and a post graduate certificate in trauma, abuse, and deprivation. He is a lifelong Pentecostal believer who was ordained by the Anglican Church in Rwanda. He has served as pastor in Nicaragua, Montreal, Arizona, and Tennessee. He has been a conference speaker in churches and colleges throughout North and South America for many years and is the author of two published books, *"Between Eden and Pandemonium"* and *"The Emerging American Church."* You can read his blog at www.christchurchnashville.org/dansthoughts.htm.

Kathy Shooster

Kathy Shooster is a praise and worship leader at Congregation Beth Yeshua in Philadelphia, PA, as well as a singer/songwriter for the internationally known Messianic choral group, Kol Simcha. She has ministered in many places, including numerous congregations, women's retreats, conferences, and outreach festivals in Russia, Ukraine, Argentina, and Israel. Kathy shares from her own life's experience in a down-to-earth manner, applying the truth of God's word to daily life. Visit Kathy online at www.kathyshooster.com.

J. Daniel Smith

Dan has produced recording projects for artists including Dámaris Carbaugh, Matthew Ward, Dennis Jernigan, Geron Davis, Wintley Phipps, Mark Condon, and many others. As a Dove Award winning arranger and orchestrator, his choral collections, octavos, and seasonal works for major publishers are myriad. For the past nineteen years Dan has produced the annual musical for the Assemblies of God World Missions. At the 2005 General Council of the Assemblies of God in Denver, Dan was inducted in the National Music Hall of Honor. He has served as Music Pastor for the past twenty-nine years at Bethesda Community Church in Fort Worth, Texas. He can be reached at dan@bethesdanet.com.

Sue Smith

Sue Smith is a three-time Dove Award winner and a staff writer with Brentwood-Benson Music Publishing in Nashville. She has had her songs recorded by Avalon, Brian Littrell, Mark Harris, Larnelle Harris, Travis Cottrell, Ernie Haase and Signature Sound, Brian Free and Assurance, Legacy V, and many others. Sue lives in St. Charles, MO, where each October, she and her husband John host the Write About Jesus Workshop for Christian songwriters (www.writeaboutjesus.com).

Angel Smythe

Angel Smythe is a recording artist and worship leader. She currently leads worship at her home church, Saddleback Church. With the release of her debut CD, "The Journey," her heart is to share the testimony of God's goodness and faithfulness in her life. Her passion is to help people find healing and wholeness in Christ and to lead them to an intimate place of worship. You can learn more about Angel at www.angelsmythe.com.

Kimberlee Stone

Kimberlee Stone is a busy woman: substitute teacher, editor, writer, speaker, party planner, valet, chef, good will ambassador, peacemaker, peacekeeper, referee, movie critic, merry maid, wife, mom. She is also an occasional speaker and author of *"I've Got A Secret."* When she isn't busy with one of her other day jobs, she's writing in her nook under the stairs. The Stone family adventures have inspired a children's series that will be finished as soon as she works out a system for sharing the computer with her pre-teen daughter. Kimberlee and Regi say they'll travel when their kids are grown, and one day she'll have a cabin in the woods or a place on the beach where she goes alone to write. But for now, picking her children up from school is the highlight of her day. You can keep up with Kimberlee at www.kimberleestone.com.

Regi Stone

As founder of Experience Worship, Regi's main priority is helping people grow to understand worship as a practical, attainable, not-*just*-musical part of their everyday lives. As owner and publisher of Belden Street Music, he produces more than 100 worship songs each year. In addition to his session work for Word, PraiseGathering, Integrity, LifeWay, Brentwood Benson and several other Christian music publishers, Regi has recorded multiple vocal projects and instrumental albums. He regularly leads worship at Christ Church in Nashville, TN as well as at conferences and churches all over the country. He and his wife Kimberlee have two children, Sophia and Eli. You can find Regi at www.registone.com.

Patrick Tharp

Patrick Tharp serves on staff as Worship Leader at Koinonia Fellowship. With a passion for musical discipleship and mentoring, Patrick heads up the Koinonia School of Worship, hosts the Worship ONE Conference, as well as producing and playing on Koinonia Praise Band's worship projects. His ministry model and motive is to do all "For the Glory of God!" He lives in upstate New York with his wife and four children. You can read more of Patrick's devotionals at www.koinoniapraiseband.com.

Appendix 3:
Additional Copyright & Works Cited

Appendix 4:
Quote Index

Appendix 5:
Author Index

EXPERIENCE WORSHIP

Information's pretty thin stuff
unless mixed with experience.

Clarence day

Experience Worship: Why We're Here

Have you been barefoot on a beach at the spot where the waves are breaking and let your feet sink into the sand? Did you ever make a mud pie as a child, or work in a garden with ungloved hands? Do you remember dancing and playing in a warm summer rain without rubber boots or a raincoat?

If you are talking to someone who has never had these experiences, the fullness is impossible to convey. You can try to explain how the sand feels squishy oozing up between your toes, or how hard it is to get dried mud out from beneath your fingernails. But you can't explain the experience, the thrill of running unprotected into the rain rather than out of it, or the dizziness you feel staring down at the tide rolling in and out over your bare feet as the ground shifts beneath you. To someone who has never experienced these things, your words only convey a concept. They haven't been there before; they don't know the feeling.

Imagine only viewing the sunset through calendar images or inspirational posters. Although they are beautiful, they are not good substitutes for the real experience. All the little, real-life details combine to form our experience of the sunset: the mugginess in the air, the sound of children playing in the yard, the fireflies beginning to glow. While it may not be as awe-inspiring as the view from the Himalayas or a Tahitian beach, we can experience it every day.

The majority of our sunsets are not meant to be epic events. They should be daily-attainable occurrences, seamless parts of our lives. Their impact lies in the fact that they are real, touch-able, smell-able, taste-able moments.

Our worship is meant to be the same. It's not only for the super spiritual who have their lives perfectly together, who never get their feet wet and never get their hands dirty. It's not confined to lofty, far-off places. It's as simple as spinning in the rain or digging our toes into the sand.

Worship is to do what we were created for, to be who we really are and share the experience with God. We don't have to climb mountains or float on clouds with harps to worship. We use what we have, where we are.

Most of us know that worship is what we were made for – but what does that really mean? Church services are not what we were made for. Singing is not the only thing we're going to be doing in eternity. Everything about the fullness of being human and how God made life to work tells us that.

Why, then, has worship become equated with singing certain songs? Why is it so hard to find people who talk about worship non-musically, let alone places where non-musical elements are recognized as expressions of worship? What can we do to expand the experience of worship? How can we make worship the palpable, reachable part of everyday life that God created us to experience?

Experience Worship exists to help answer those questions. We're here to find practical ways to free worship from belonging exclusively in a musical context, to learn to *live* worship – not just talk and sing about living it – and to help people learn to do the same.

Experience Worship is about helping believers become truly aware that the presence of God is right where we are all the time – doing the dishes, playing in the sandbox with our kids, driving our car, working our inglorious jobs. God is not sitting in some faraway place. His presence is right where we are, all day, every day. If God is there, we can experience worship.

We think this is really, really important. That's why we're here.

Do you have perspectives on worship that you would like to share?
Any thoughts, ideas or questions about worship as a practical, attainable,
not-*just*-musical experience meant for real people living in the real world?

www.experienceworship.com

Join the conversation.